FIT *to* PRINT

FIT *to* PRINT

The Canadian Student's Guide to Essay Writing

SECOND EDITION

Joanne Buckley

University of Western Ontario

Harcourt Brace Jovanovich

Toronto   Orlando   San Diego   London   Sydney

Copyright © 1991
Harcourt Brace Jovanovich Canada Inc.
All rights reserved

Canadian Cataloguing in Publication Data

Buckley, Joanne Lorna, 1953-
  Fit to print

2nd ed.
ISBN 0-7747-3144-3

1. Report writing.   2. English language — Rhetoric.
I. Title.

LB2369.B83 1991   808'.02   C90-094480-3

Acquisitions Editor: Heather McWhinney
Developmental Editor: Jean Underwood
Managing Editor: Liz Radojkovic
Editorial Co-ordinator: Marcel Chiera
Editorial Assistant: Kerry Gibson
Copy Editor: Beverley Beetham Endersby
Cover and Interior Design: Jack Steiner Graphic Design
Cover Illustration: Peter Nagy
Typesetting and Assembly: Computer Composition of Canada, Inc.
Printing and Binding: John Deyell Company

Printed in Canada

1 2 3 4 5   95 94 93 92 91

Contents

Preface

The second edition of *Fit to Print* maintains the book's original focus on the problems of essay writing experienced by most students today at the university, college, and secondary levels. It is intended for use not only as a textbook for writing courses, but also as a supplementary guide in the humanities and social sciences. It emphasizes the different types of essays across the curriculum, such as the research essay, the essay exam, and the book review.

While still offering practical guidelines on how to organize an essay and to address specific difficulties in grammar and style, the second edition incorporates some major changes.

1. Expansion of the documentation section to include University of Chicago style, preferred by most history instructors.
2. More information about the APA style of documentation.
3. More specific advice to the student on how to develop a thesis statement and begin the process of essay writing.
4. An expanded chapter on paragraphing, with more examples and more material on writing good topic sentences.
5. A more thorough discussion of the revision process.
6. A new sample research essay.
7. A checklist of revision symbols on the inside front cover.
8. An expanded chapter on parts of the sentence.
9. New exercises and more examples throughout.
10. Improved organization of chapters, a more thorough index, and an updated appendix for use as a reference.

This edition of *Fit to Print* has been reorganized so that the discussion of tone is introduced earlier, and the information on elements of style later, after a discussion of sentence mechanics, in Part V. Writing teachers who use this text have suggested these changes to assist students in using it as a self-help guide.

The strengths of the first edition of *Fit to Print* remain:

1. The text provides a sequential approach to help students in the process of essay organization and craftsmanship.
2. It presents readable lessons and exercises on specific common grammatical and stylistic problems.
3. It draws on student examples and deals with essay assignments across disciplines.
4. The text is Canadian in its authorship and its examples.
5. The tone of the text is lively and not condescending.
6. The book may be adapted for use as a self-help guide and as a classroom text.

Fit to Print, in its second edition, stresses that writing involves a positive relationship between reader and writer. The goal for both student and instructor is writing that makes a good impression.

■ Publisher's Note to Instructors and Students

This textbook is a key component of your course. If you are the instructor of this course, you undoubtedly considered a number of texts carefully before choosing this as the one that will work best for your students and you. The authors and publishers of this book spent considerable time and money to ensure its high quality, and we appreciate your recognition of this effort and accomplishment.

If you are a student, we are confident that this text will help you to meet the objectives of your course. You will also find it helpful after the course is finished, as a valuable addition to your personal library. So hold on to it.

As well, please don't forget that photocopying copyright work means the authors lose royalties that are rightfully theirs. This loss will discourage them from writing another edition of this text or other books, because doing so will simply not be worth their time and effort. If this happens, we all lose — students, instructors, authors, and publishers.

Acknowledgements

The second edition of *Fit to Print* owes its existence to a number of people: first, to my students whose questions, and answers to my questions, serve as inspiration; next, to my reviewers, William Benzie, Robert Campbell, Dianne Edwards, Karen Jakob, Susan Lieberman, Jim MacDonald, Mary O'Connor, and Douglas Owram for their helpful suggestions for the improvement of the text; third, to my editors, Heather McWhinney, Jean Underwood, Sandra Peltier, Liz Radojkovic, Marcel Chiera, Kerry Gibson, and the copy editor Beverley Endersby, who made painstaking and necessary changes; and last, to the instructors who use *Fit to Print* at The University of Western Ontario and who kindly gave me advice about revisions. Thanks also to my parents and David Gates, for countless things.

Introduction— Defining the Essay

> Essays do, in a way, resemble scientific writing;
> they report experiments in thought.
>
> *Lewis Thomas*

◼ If at First You Don't Succeed . . .

The essay, as any dictionary will tell you, is an attempt. This definition itself ought to be reassuring if you have ever worried about how you would be able to write an essay. You can't fail as long as what you write is a sincere attempt to come to terms with a particular subject. The finished essay succeeds insofar as it is an honest attempt to elucidate some aspect of your topic.

An essay need not fail as long as your ideas are treated fairly, honestly, and in a spirit of thorough and intensive investigation—and you have communicated these ideas to the reader! If the essay seems an especially burdensome assignment, it may be because most of us are not accustomed to independent thought. Try to think of the essay as an opportunity to stretch your intellectual muscles and to think your own thoughts.

To write an essay is to engage in a creative process, to bring an idea to life. The essay itself, however, is a finished product, not a record of the process by which you wrote it.

Whether you are writing an expository essay (meant to explain something), or a persuasive essay (meant to argue something), the essay's chief purpose is to present a thesis that focusses your ideas and conveys them to the reader in a way that shows their worth and their validity. Depending on the occasion, an essay may be formal or informal; however, academic writing usually demands formality. Depending on the nature of the assignment, the essay may be a product of reasoning or of a combination of reasoning and research.

This text deals both with the essentials of essay writing and with the variations expected in different kinds of assignments. Skim its contents first to acquaint yourself with the most important steps of essay writing. If you are unfamiliar with the basic requirements of the essay, pay special attention to Parts I, II, and III. If you are unsure of the specific guidelines for a particular kind of essay, check the pertinent section in Part IV. Then, as you write your next essay, use this book as a step-by-step guide. It will provide helpful suggestions on how to organize your thinking, and how to present your material in the most effective manner.

Remember that the essay is an attempt to think through your ideas in a structured way. Each attempt will teach you more about how the process works for you.

■ Try, Try Again

As you plan and write the essay, you will be trying various ideas on for size. The process of writing an essay involves finding some part of a large topic that fits your attitude toward and interest in the subject. Compromise is essential. The essay must fit both you and the topic: it will show you and the reader what you know and what you have yet to learn. For best results, choose a topic in which you have some personal stake. Make sure that you can treat the topic satisfactorily within the required word limit and within the time constraints of the assignment.

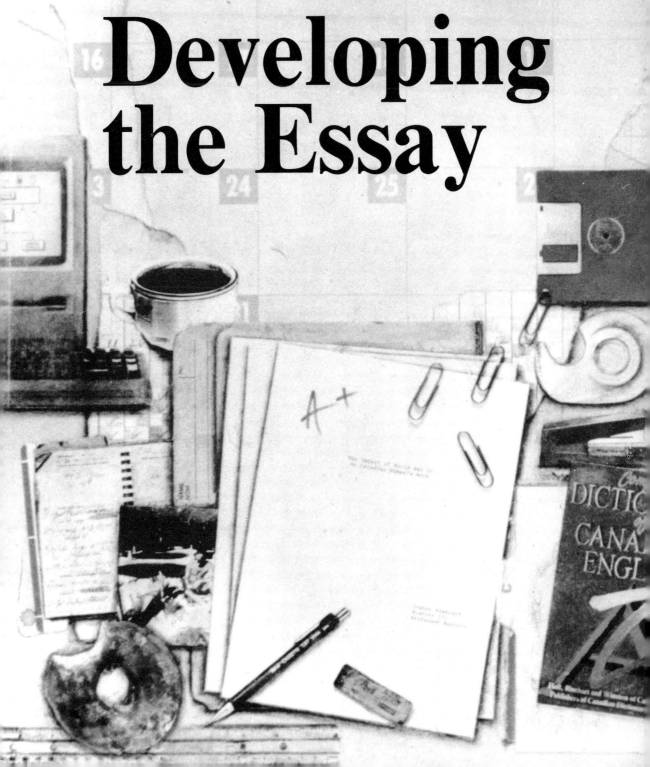

PART ONE

Developing the Essay

Devising a Thesis

The art of writing has for backbone some fierce attachment to an idea.

Virginia Woolf

Usually when you begin to write an essay, you will have in mind a broad area of concentration or a fundamental topic that you mean to explore. To write a successful essay, you must find the focal point of your discussion — the centre of your thought, from which the points you make may radiate outward. This focal point is the thesis statement.

Topics are only the starting point for your thinking. They tell you only the general area of investigation. Whether a topic is given to you by the instructor or whether you find your own, the topic must be narrowed down to serve as the focus of your paper. Like the bull's eye in the middle of a dartboard, the thesis statement is the centre that holds your argument together. An essay succeeds because the point to be made is directly on target, and the significance of the point is firmly established.

■ Discovering a Topic

If your instructor has not suggested areas for exploration, you will have to create your own, usually subject to his or her approval. This process need not be drudgery; it gives you the opportunity to explore your own interest in the subject.

The following are some suggestions for finding a general topic or area of interest:

1. Skim the index and table of contents of any book mentioned in class as a useful source.
2. Skim through class notes and text for ideas that catch your imagination.
3. Ask questions about the meaning and value of the subject.

Always write down ideas as you go along.

■ Shopping for a Thesis Statement

Often, you will be given a general topic and be instructed to narrow it down. Remember, though, a topic is only a general idea in need of development.

Suppose you were asked in an Administrative Studies course to write an essay of 2500–3000 words about productivity growth in Japan. Obviously, this is a broad subject that could yield several promising thesis statements. By itself, however, it is just a phrase and makes no meaningful statement. Keep this example in mind as you read through the following tips on developing a specific thesis statement.

Consider the writing situation

When you develop a topic, keep these determining factors in mind:

1. your interests, strengths, and weaknesses
2. the reader's expectations
3. the restrictions of the assignment

Use whatever you have at your disposal

1. supplemental bibliographies you may have been given
2. advice from the instructor
3. material from the course itself
4. your native wit
5. library materials—books, journals, and audio-visual materials

Ask questions about the general topic

Your first question with regard to our sample topic might be "What about it?" Your sources, both in class and out, may have revealed to you that Japanese productivity growth has greatly surpassed that of Canada since World War II.

Your next question might be "Why?", suggesting a cause-and-effect development, or even "How?", suggesting an argument based on classification (the breakdown of ideas into categories) or on process (the orderly presentation of steps). Refer also to Chapter 4 for some suggested approaches to topic development.

Consider your topic in conjunction with something else

Try joining your topic to these conjunctions: "and," "or," "but," "so." These linking words should give you some idea of what might be productively attached to your topic to yield interesting results.

"And," for example, might help you think of things that can be compared (or contrasted) with your subject: Japanese productivity and Canadian productivity, for instance.

"Or" might lead you to consider a controversy about the causes of Japanese productivity: advanced technology or employee motivation, for example.

"But" might allow you to refute the position of a particular authority on the subject, or to prove that the rate of productivity growth in Japan's case is more a result of the stage of its industrial development than of superior technology or administration.

Consider key words that form part of the topic

Ask yourself about the nuances of the question or topic for discussion: is there ambiguity or potential for development in the wording of the question? When setting questions, instructors usually have only a sketchy idea in mind; try to see in the topic as much as or more than they have.

In our sample general topic, one word to which this tactic might apply is "productivity." To develop your topic, you might investigate what particular areas are most productive, to find a clue for your response. You might also want to explore exactly what is meant by "growth." Does it mean increased profits, expansion in number of products, or development of new products?

Consult your own taste

Your taste in topics should be consulted before you settle on anything. About the only serious mistake you can make is to choose a topic simply because it looks easier than the others. A challenge is often the best choice since it allows you to ponder the topic rather than assuming, probably incorrectly, that the main point is clear or the answer obvious.

Try on the topic before you decide

Always play with the topic before you work on it. Play with ideas by scratching them down haphazardly on a sheet of paper without regard (for now) to problems of order or clarity. This kind of unstructured thinking will open up the possibilities of the question or the topic for you in a way that no amount of tidy compartmentalizing can.

Brainstorm by writing ideas down

1. Try clustering ideas together according to their associations for you.
2. Try drawing diagrams, connecting various ideas.
3. Check the meanings of words in the topic, and perhaps even their etymologies, for clues to the direction you should take.

■ A Working Thesis vs. a Polished Thesis Statement

If you follow the guidelines above, you should be able to arrive at a narrow focus for your paper. But even a thesis statement should be subject to revision. Because it is normally part of the introduction to a paper, writers often mistakenly assume that it should be written first. In fact, your real thesis statement may emerge only after you have made several false starts.

Since you have to start somewhere, begin with a working thesis. It will allow you to consider your material from a tentative point of view. If you find that the evidence begins to contradict it, or you no longer consider it the centre of your discussion, redefine your statement to suit the new circumstances.

The thesis statement that appears in your finished introduction will be the best description of what you are trying to prove and of how you propose to do it. For example, your thesis statement on the subject of Japanese productivity growth might look like this:

The enormous increase recorded in productivity growth in Japan in the past ten years is largely the result of new theories of employee relations that have been developed in Japanese industry.

Look before you leap

Once you have formulated a contention, that is, some idea of what your approach to the topic is going to be, you must formulate a thesis statement, along with some sense of the essay's ultimate direction. You may want to visit the library to take note of what relevant books and journal articles are available on your specific subject, and of whether they support or contradict your working thesis.

To write a good thesis statement, you need to remember that a strong thesis is a contention that forms the basis of your argument. It is what you are trying to show the reader. A good thesis statement takes into account the purpose of the writing and its audience, but it does more than that. For instance, your purpose might be to define for a beginner the perfect golf swing. Although this idea shows promise, it is not a thesis statement. To transform it, you need to make a claim. Look at this statement:

A perfect golf swing demands a proper grip, delicate balance, and excellent timing.

It is a strong thesis statement because it makes a claim that the rest of the essay, presumably, will go on to support.

Suppose, now, that your topic is "learning a foreign language." Your purpose is to tell your reader what you consider the best way to learn a language. You must not, however, leave the topic too vague. Instead, you might compose a thesis statement like the following:

The best way to learn a foreign language is through active practice and immersion among native speakers.

This thesis is stronger than, say, one that argues that learning a foreign language is difficult because this one is contentious: some might, after all, disagree and claim that study and reading are more important than practice and immersion. It is your job to make your case convincingly.

■ What to Look for in a Thesis Statement

Personal conviction

No writing of any power is ever possible without commitment to the subject. No motivation is ever as pressing as the need to say something on a subject that matters urgently to you. Your first task is to find an approach to the topic capable of moving you to care and to work and to write. If you can find such an approach, the process of writing—the reading, the thinking, even the reworking of your thoughts—will be carried along by the desire to know and not only by the need to complete the assignment.

Pertinence

An essay should not be a trivial pursuit. It should matter to you and to its reader. As you shape your thesis statement, keep the *value* of your subject in mind. When selecting a point of view, allow yourself to think about its broader implications, even if there is no place to include all of these in the essay itself. You don't have to tell readers how relevant your topic is, but you should believe it, and you should be able to show that you do. Ensuring that your perspective is new and making your point of view matter to your reader are fundamental requirements.

Proportion

The thesis statement indicates what size the essay will be in its finished form. A well-measured thesis statement is snug, not loose, in its fit. If it does not fit properly, the arguments that follow may sag. To ensure a good fit between thesis statement and essay, ask questions. Ask yourself if there is room in a 1500-word essay to discuss all the implications of the Meech Lake Accord. If not, then trim the thesis statement to fit: e.g., The role of Bourassa in the Meech Lake Accord.

Precision

As in a legal contract, the essay is the delivery of promises made in its thesis statement. And, as with all such contracts, the issues to be dealt with must be clarified at the outset. Make sure before you develop your thesis statement that you have made clear to your readers both what your essay will do *and* what it will *not* do. Feel free to announce (without apologies) in or near the thesis statement what the limits of your treatment of the subject are.

Point

Not only should your thesis statement have a point to make, it must point in a particular direction. A useful addition to the thesis statement itself is the "route map." The route map informs readers of the highlights of the journey they are about to make. For instance, in a sociology essay comparing the changing attitudes toward women in advertisements from the 1940s to the 1980s, as reflected in two issues of the same magazine, you can briefly outline the steps in your discussion:

> *Three major changes can be noted in the presentation of female figures: women are shown less often in domestic situations; women are more often featured as authority figures; and women are more often shown in active, rather than passive, roles.*

Such a statement contains the direction of the entire essay in miniature and points toward the arguments to follow.

Now that you have a thesis statement . . .

Use your thesis statement as the springboard for the outline. Keep it in mind as you develop your thought. With your thesis statement on paper, you are now ready to set the tone for the readers you have in mind.

EXERCISES

1. Develop a focus for the following topics, using some of the techniques listed above. *Hint*: Each is meant to be the subject of a 1500-word essay in the discipline suggested.

    a. the treatment of the aged (Sociology)
    b. the fall of the Berlin Wall (Political Science)
    c. women novelists (English)
    d. the career of a sports hero (Physical Education)
    e. kinds of leadership (Administrative Studies)
    f. exploitation of native peoples (History)
    g. free will and destiny (Philosophy)
    h. TV commercials and consumerism (Sociology)
    i. the role of women in the epic (Classical Studies)
    j. the implications of *glasnost* (Political Science)

2. Examine some of your past essays to see if the thesis statements you have written have narrowed the topic down sufficiently. Try rewriting them to give them more focus.

3. Develop a thesis statement for each of the following topics:

    a. the importance of leisure time
    b. working part-time
    c. having discipline
    d. eating habits
    e. your attitude toward fashion
    f. investing
    g. reform in education
    h. pet care
    i. your worst fears
    j. what really matters in life

Setting Tone

No one can write decently who is distrustful of the reader's intelligence, or whose attitude is patronizing.

E.B. White

Tone is one of the most elusive features of a writing style, whether your own or someone else's. The tone of your essay writing, if it is to avoid clashing with the reader's expectations, should be neither too loud nor too soft. Harsh tones may antagonize your readers. Conversely, gentle tones may make your arguments seem too weak or too bland.

Tone in writing may be compared to tone of voice. It is the personality of an essay. What follows will show both which tones to avoid and which to emulate. When you read your paper aloud to check for errors at the revision stage, you will listen for potential problems. But even before you write, it is important to think about the impact of your ideas on the readers.

The tone you choose must fit the purposes of your essay. If the assignment is a formal research paper, the tone must be appropriately formal as well. If, on the other hand, you are writing an informal, more personal paper, your tone may be correspondingly more casual. The expectations of your readers define the tone for you.

In large part, setting tone is a process of audience analysis. In order to communicate with your audience effectively, your writing must show that it takes the reader's reactions seriously. Some of the preparation you go through to write an essay necessarily involves anticipation of how your audience is likely to react to your subject. When you have thought about the potential problems, you are ready to set the tone of your paper.

■ Tones to Avoid

Avoid whispering

A tone that is too "soft" suggests that the writer is unsure of the words and the thoughts behind them. Words that are too tentative, too hesitant, are one sign of a whispering tone. Phrases like "it seems to be" or "perhaps" or "it could be that" are indications of the problem. Another signal is the overuse of qualifying phrases such as "however" and "to some extent." Although some qualifications are a good idea, too many may cause the reader to doubt your confidence in your own position.

Avoid chatting

A chatty essay is most often the result of incomplete planning and outlining. If your paragraphs or your sentences seem to trail off or to lead to unexpected conclusions, if your ideas seem linked by random association, if your language seems too colloquial or offhand, and if you treat the reader as a chum rather than as an interested observer, you may be accused of chattiness. The cure for chattiness is care, revision, and a polite, though distanced, regard for the reader.

Avoid emotiveness

An emotive tone is struck when a writer attempts to describe his or her feelings in a high-flown, exaggerated way. Often, what results sounds falsely sentimental or hackneyed. Such a tone is often found in introductions and conclusions, particularly when a writer tries to wax poetic about his or her opinions. Although opinions are warranted in an essay, it is nevertheless not necessary to praise Shakespeare as a great playwright at the end of a paper analyzing the structure of *Macbeth*, or to tell the reader of an essay on nuclear disarmament that the issue is a matter of life and death for the human race. Show your feelings by supporting your opinions; don't just declare them.

Avoid declaiming

Treat your reader as an equal. Though you may well be playing the role of expert, your role is to reason with your reader and to assume his or her rationality. Any style that repeats points too often, or goes on too long, or explains more than the reader needs is declaiming. This tactic, in combination with a pretentious vocabulary, is disastrous. When you revise, check to see that your writing is transparent, that it does not need to be deciphered to be understood. Avoid words that intimidate the reader because of their length or their obscurity. Choose instead the word that will most clearly express your meaning. Check also to see that the essay is within the required word limit.

In a formal essay, it is also wise to limit the use of rhetorical questions, or to avoid them altogether. Your job is to tell the reader something, not to ask questions.

Avoid shouting

Make sure that your essay does not inadvertently antagonize its readers. Even though it is your job to defend your viewpoint, you must not assume that your readers are opponents. This problem with tone is especially prevalent in essays that attempt to refute someone else's position. In these cases, the force should be in the logic of your argument, rather than in the tone of your writing.

Use personal pronouns with discretion

Avoid directly addressing your reader in formal essays. "You" and "your" may alienate the readers if your assumptions about their knowledge or their attitudes are incorrect. It may even sound cheeky or overbearing. If you can, keep the readers on your side; if you know they disagree, keep them at a formal distance.

A research or formal expository essay also may demand that you avoid the use of "I" in writing. If you are forbidden the use of "I" by an instructor, respect that condition.

Do, however, try to avoid awkward impersonal constructions and self-conscious references. Never refer to yourself as "the writer" or "the author."

On the other hand, if "I" is acceptable, *use* it. Your relationship to your reader in a formal essay is meant to be a professional one, but that does not mean that personality has no place, simply that you must know its place, and respect the polite distance imposed between you and the reader.

Example

    X It is the opinion of this writer that . . . (too stuffy)
    X In my opinion . . . (too weakly subjective)

    ✔ *This paper contends that . . .*
    ✔ *I will show that . . .*

 ## Tones to Emulate

Modulate your writing style

A modulated voice is controlled. Despite the moods of the writer, it shows restraint, politeness, and judgment. Your tones in private conversation may be more varied; in the essay, however (except in the freer personal essay), your tone should be cool, professional, unruffled, and firm.

Imitate the best

Read newspaper editorials and news magazines, as well as your fellow students' essays. Textbooks and critical material may also serve as examples, though you must choose with discretion. And listen. The tone of classroom lectures is often a good indication of what is expected in a paper.

EXERCISE

Find an essay in a learned journal and analyze its tone. Do the same with an article in a popular magazine. Describe the tone of both pieces. How do the works differ in terms of audience and purpose? Compare them in terms of vocabulary, use of personal pronouns, use of specialized language, complexity of sentence structure, and assumptions about the reader's familiarity with and interest in the subject under discussion. How is the tone, whether formal or informal, created in each case?

PART TWO

Designing the Essay

Designing an Outline

How do I know what I think until I see what I say?

E.M. Forster

Once you have decided upon your topic, determined your thesis statement, and considered your audience and purpose, you need an outline.

Never attempt to write an essay without some kind of outline — whether it be a formal, detailed itinerary or a hastily jotted map showing your destination, your direction, and the stops you wish to make along the way.

When preparing an outline, remember that it is only a sketch of your paper. The final design of the essay may be quite different from what you originally intended. A sketch does not need to be perfect. The outline is meant to help you write the paper, not to restrict your line of thought. Keep the outline flexible so that you can tinker with it as you go along. It is simply a tentative blueprint, a description of the contents of your paper, rather than a prescription of its requirements.

■ Make a Table of Contents

Think of the outline as your own flexible table of contents. It is, after all, your note to yourself, your reminder of what details you wish to include and what arguments you want to make. Like a table of contents, the outline labels what the reader may expect to find contained in the work itself.

Take a look at the table of contents of this book for a moment to see what information can be gleaned from it. Not only does it tell you *what* is included in the book, it tells you what the major and minor divisions of the work are. For instance, you will find the chapter entitled "Devising a Thesis" under the part heading "Developing the Essay."

In other words, the table of contents gives the reader a sense of the book's dimensions. You see, for example, that the book you are holding in your hand has six major parts, each of which is divided into a number of chapters. Thus, it gives you a sense not only of the work's overall shape, but also of the size of each component, and, at the same time, of the orderly arrangement of its position within the work. What follows is not a set of rules for composing outlines, but a series of suggestions about what they may contain.

To make your outline as useful and as organized as a table of contents, keep the following steps in mind:

■ Sort Through Your Ideas

1. Make sure you have established your pivotal points: the thesis statement and purpose.

Use your thesis statement (subject to revision) and your selected purpose as the launching points for your outline. From them will emanate all the ideas, arguments, facts, and figures you have gathered.

2. Gather your notes.

With your tentative thesis statement on paper in front of you, gather your tentative remarks, your research, and your questions about the topic. One good way to take notes is to list separate ideas on index cards (remembering to include sources, if any). This way, you can shuffle or discard material easily.

Keeping your purpose in mind, organize the material you have selected, discarding any information not strictly related to it. If you are discussing kinds of stage props, for instance, don't include material on their development in the history of the theatre.

3. Classify your material.

Decide how many steps your argument contains. Then classify your notes accordingly. If, for example, you mean to consider three reasons that Japanese businesses outrank their Canadian counterparts, decide in which of the three discussions to include a statistic about productivity growth.

4. Order your material in a logical way.

This process demands that you decide at what point a particular argument should be mentioned. Here you must decide what your opening argument, your follow up, and your last word should be. Keep in mind the tried-and-true notion that a strong point is best placed at the beginning or ending of an essay. Keep in mind, too, that some of your organizational decisions are dependent upon the pattern of argument you selected at the outset. If you know, for instance, that your reader will need to understand your definition of a crown corporation to get the most out of your essay, put it where it will be most accessible. Of, if you are explaining a process, make sure the reader is able to follow it step by step.

5. Rank your points according to their importance.

Sorting your ideas according to rank means deciding whether an item has a major role or merely a minor one to play. The ranking itself will give you an excellent idea of what you have to say and of how developed your thought is. Where you have much to add or to explain, the idea is vital and may serve as a significant part of your argument; where your idea is almost all you have to say on the subject, you may relegate the point to a minor status.

In order to rank your ideas, assign them numbers or letters, beginning perhaps with capital Roman numerals for major sections, moving to capital letters for important supporting sections, through to Arabic numbers for less important support material, to small letters for the minor details. The points you are making are primary in rank; the support you gather for them is secondary.

6. Invent a title.

Although you still have not arrived at a finished product, the argument you make in your essay should be clear enough to you that a title should pose no problem. Just bear in mind that a title should give the reader specific information about the subject you are writing about. Don't entitle your paper "Margaret Atwood"; instead, call it "The Function of Autobiographical Form in Atwood's *Cat's Eye*." Do not underline your title; reserve underlining for the titles of published works. A title should be catchy and not too lengthy, but don't sacrifice clarity for flourish.

Example

I. Japan outranks Canada in productivity for two reasons.
  A. Japanese companies are especially concerned with employee relations. (REASON # 1)
    1. Employees are often hired for life, not for limited periods, as often is done in Canada.
    2. Employees are given greater benefits and security than in Canadian companies.
      a. They are encouraged to participate in decisions more often than is the case in Canada.
      b. Their jobs are usually more stable than ours, though lower wages are sometimes the result.
      c. Japanese workers are treated like family members, rather than as employees.
  B. Japanese companies place special emphasis on technological advancements. (REASON # 2)
    1. Technological advancement has permitted more efficient quality control.
      a. "Computerized" and "robotized" assembly lines have decreased the margin of error.

The form of notation does not matter particularly, but it should permit you to see *at a glance* the relative scope of the point you are making. A carefully ranked outline will show you the ideas within ideas.

■ Tailor the Outline

As you outline, you may well notice some rags and tatters among your notes, bits of research material that seemed valuable at the time you took the notes, though they now seem unrelated to the development of your thought. If you cannot use these scraps in the final fabric of your argument, do not hesitate to toss them out. Remember that one of the main functions of the outline is to show you how well the material you have gathered actually fits the viewpoint you have chosen. Each point of the outline ought to represent an area that you can fill with developed thoughts, facts, and evidence. If you find that all you have to say on a particular point can be fleshed out in one sentence, then you must find a way to incorporate that small point into another place in your argument or perhaps you may have to eliminate it altogether. What isn't useful or appropriate for your thesis statement should be left behind.

The outline below shows a short persuasive essay developed by examples, definition, classification, and even comparison/contrast. Basically, the essay consists of three arguments to defend the thesis, plus supporting arguments. These patterns of argument will be discussed in the next chapter.

Note that each section has a small thesis statement (or topic sentence) of its own. These are best written as sentences in the outline to ensure clarity. Note also that the subdivisions allow you to see at a glance what items have the most support (and conversely, what might be in need of greater support or development).

A sample student outline

TOPIC: Headaches
PATTERN OF ARGUMENT: Classification

I. INTRODUCTION: Everyone suffers a headache at one time or another, though the pain can vary in degree. Some headaches respond to aspirin; others are excruciating, perhaps chronic or debilitating.
THESIS STATEMENT: In order to treat a headache properly, one must be able to diagnose it correctly.
PREVIEW: There are four types of headache: the tension headache, the cluster headache, the sinus headache, and the migraine.

II. BODY
  A. A tension headache
    a. Cause: muscle contraction
    b. Symptoms: dull, steady ache, tightness around the scalp or neck
    c. Triggers: stress, anxiety, repressed emotion
    d. Treatment: aspirin
  B. A cluster headache
    a. Cause: unknown
    b. Symptoms: burning, piercing pain, often behind one eye; occurs periodically for days, weeks, or months; less than an hour in duration
    c. Triggers: smoking, alcohol consumption, histamines, or nitroglycerine
    d. Treatment: medication, such as ergotamines, inhaled or held under the tongue
  C. A sinus headache
    a. Cause: any disturbances blocking the passage of fluid from the sinuses
    b. Symptoms: gnawing pain, rise in temperature
    c. Triggers: same as cause
    d. Treatment: nasal decongestants and antibiotics
  D. A migraine
    a. Cause: not known

b. Symptoms: nausea, dizziness, cold hands, tremor, sensitivity to light and sound; sometimes a day of longer in duration

c. Triggers: irregular eating and sleeping; ingestion of cheese, chocolate, red wine, or caffeine

d. Treatment: no cure, but some medications prevent or abort headaches; lifestyle changes are recommended

III. CONCLUSION: Relief from headaches is possible for most people if they learn to seek the safest and most effective treatment available.

EXERCISES

1. Develop outlines, complete with thesis statements, for the following topics:
   a. the home-video industry
   b. AIDS education
   c. street crime
   d. women clergy
   e. collecting things
   f. family breakdowns
   g. private schools
   h. the cost of education

2. Reread an essay you have written for a course in the past and sketch an outline of its structure. Is each section clearly delineated? Is adequate support given for each point that you raise? Is the movement of the paper logical and easy to follow? Would you do anything differently in light of the outline you have produced?

3. Read an essay you find in a journal related to your field of study. Make an outline of it, complete with thesis statement, arguments, and support.

Choosing a Pattern of Argument

> Everywhere I go I'm asked if I think the universities stifle writers. My opinion is that they don't stifle enough of them. There's many a best-seller that could have been prevented by a good teacher.
>
> *Flannery O'Connor*

After you have established your thesis statement and made your outline, you need to choose the pattern or patterns of argument that will do it justice. Usually an essay will demand several patterns in support of its thesis, as the sample outline in the preceding chapter demonstrates. In order to support your thesis with a similar variety of arguments, you must look for methods by which to direct your thought. The following tactics may serve as structural guidelines or blueprints for your thought:

Definition/Description
Example
Classification
Comparison/Contrast
Cause/Effect
Narration

These patterns cannot be entirely separated from each other. Usually, a writer will use several patterns to develop one essay. Refer, for example, to the outline in the preceding chapter. It uses many different kinds of argument, including definition, classification, comparison/contrast, and example.

A paragraph that defines "dreams," for example, may contrast a simple dictionary definition with a more elaborate definition offered by a psychologist. Examples of dreams may be given to show something about their essential nature, perhaps demonstrating the creativity of the unconscious mind.

The patterns listed below should offer you some inspiration when you get stuck in the process of outlining your thought. Refer to this section when you need help in the amplification of an argument.

■ Definition/Description

Definition suggests the use of a dictionary to define a term explicitly. This tactic ensures that there is a general consensus between writer and readers as to the term's meaning in the context of the essay.

Although dictionary definitions are important, don't rely too heavily on them. Belabouring a definition already familiar to your readers may alienate them: it may sound condescending. Furthermore, a critical reader will be concerned more with what you *make* of a definition than with its content per se. If you do cite a dictionary definition, make sure that you use it to make a point.

What comprises a useful definition? First, it must supply the reader with characteristics that describe something. Occasionally, it may describe by way of comparison/contrast, by showing what the thing is not. And, it may give some enlightening history of the term, showing how it came to have the meaning it has. It may then show what something does, in order to describe more concretely what it is. Lastly, it may give an example, meant to epitomize the nature of the thing described.

Example

What, exactly, is a dream? Webster's *says nothing more than that it is a "hallucination in sleep."[1] This rather bland attempt at definition masks the essential problem. The truth is that we do not really know what dreams are, though there has always been a great deal of speculation about their nature. Some modern psychologists, such as Carl Jung, maintain that dreams are unconscious subjective re-creations of reality: "the dream is the theater where the dreamer is at once scene, actor, prompter, stage manager, author, audience, and critic."[2] But, even among modern psychologists, there is still considerable disagreement about the source of dreams.*

This definition introduces the subject and provides two possible definitions of what dreams are.

■ Example

Because readers usually find it easier to understand what they can picture, examples are often the best means of amplifying an argument. Whether you use an extended example, meant to illustrate your general point in a series of specific ways, or whether you use a variety of small examples to achieve the same end, examples lend support to your argument.

Example

One of the most famous recorded dreams is Kekulé's account of his discovery of the nature of benzene. In 1865, Kekulé, a chemist, fell asleep and dreamt of a snake with its tail in its mouth.[3] His intuition about the structure of benzene—that its molecules were not open structures but rings—was one of the cornerstones of modern scientific thinking. This episode illustrates that some dreams have a creative component capable of communicating, in a flash, something that the conscious mind has been seeking in vain. Some dreams apparently can bring about a breakthrough in understanding.

This example supports the idea that dreams are sometimes creative.

■ Classification

In order to explain something more precisely, a writer often has recourse to methods of classification, by which he or she can make necessary distinctions within a subject area. Classifying different parts of a subject involves making decisions about what belongs where. A large subject may be divided into smaller or more manageable sections to make important distinctions clear. In order for classification to work convincingly, the reader must be assured that the categories are tidy, include everything essential, and do not substantially overlap.

Example

> *Although dreams have been a subject of much study throughout history, there is still no consensus about what dreams mean. Some philosophers, like Bertrand Russell, contend that dreams cannot be differentiated from reality, that, in fact, we do not know which is real, the waking state or the dreaming state.[4] Others maintain, even in certain modern cultures, that dreams have divinatory qualities that tell us something about what might happen. Modern psychologists argue that dreams are proof of unconscious activity in the mind, and their studies of dreams seek to understand the springs of behaviour.*

This classification lists some of the different interpretations of what dreams mean.

■ Process

It is often necessary in the course of an essay to explain how to do something or how something works. When describing a process, think of yourself as a teacher. It is part of your job to supply your readers with all the information they require to understand, without confusion, a given process. At the same time, you must be careful to assess their level of understanding accurately, if you are to avoid writing that is boring or condescending. It is also part of your job to present the material in a logical step-by-step manner, so that the reader is spared needless cross-referencing and rereading. Check your description of the process to see if its steps can be easily followed.

Example

> *The Freudian view of the process of dreaming, recorded in* The Interpretation of Dreams *in 1899, suggests that dreams are stimulated by bodily reactions, experiences during daylight hours, and infantile memories. When people dream, according to Freud, they give way to primitive impulses, to repressed wishes, often displaced or represented in symbolic terms. When they awaken, dreamers revise their dreams by rationalizing and elaborating upon their reports of them. To understand these subconscious processes, Freud suggested that the content of dreams be analyzed through free association that would allow the dreamer to become aware of the hidden meanings and symbols of the dream.[5]*

This paragraph outlines the steps in Freud's interpretation of the process of dreaming.

Comparison/Contrast

Comparisons are an essential part of expository writing. No pattern of argument is more common on examination questions, for instance, than comparison/contrast.

A comparison includes both similarities and differences. When you contrast, however, you focus exclusively on the differences between things.

When comparing, keep the overall structure in mind. You may present first one thing and then the other, or you may present the two things in combination. Alternating between the two is best if the material to be covered is complex or lengthy.

Example

From earliest times, there has been sharp disagreement about the sources of dreams. One school of thought sees dreams as a natural phenomenon; the other sees them as something supernatural. Even the basic division between Freud and Jung on the nature of dreams can be seen this way. Freud holds that dreams are explainable in terms of what he calls "day residue" and of external stimuli;[6] that is, they are borrowed from the images of daily life accompanied by bodily disturbances. Together these elements produce a dream that reveals much about the dreamer's repressed desires and feelings. Jung's account of the source of dreams is more spiritual and less a part of natural human functions. He argues that a "dream is the small hidden door in the deepest and most intimate sanctum of the soul"[7] and his studies of individuals' dreams attempt to relate the dreamer to the larger patterns of human consciousness throughout history.

This paragraph illustrates the main differences between Jung and Freud on the subject of dreams.

Cause and Effect

This pattern traces the relationship between the cause of an event or a condition and its results. When seeking to develop an argument by tracing causes and their effects, keep in mind two potential dangers. First, beware of trusting the idea of causality too much. Simply because one thing follows another chronologically does not mean that the second event was caused by the first.

Second, do not limit effects to one cause alone. Usually more than one determinant brings about an event or a trend. Don't wear blinkers in your zeal to establish connections.

Example

Recent studies show that there is a physiological correlation between sleep patterns and the frequency of dreams. In the 1950s, researchers found a link between bursts of rapid eye movement (sometimes called REM sleep), increased electrical activity in the brain, and frequency of reported dreams. If a dreamer is awakened during a period of REM sleep, there is a much greater chance that he or she will report and remember a dream. These studies show that dreams usually, though not always, occur in conjunction with certain patterns of activity in the dreamer's brain.[8]

This paragraph points out a relationship between sleep patterns and dreams. It also illustrates one of the problems in establishing an argument; note that while the author of the paragraph does mention a correlation between two things, there is no claim of a definite cause-and-effect relation between them. Often, there can be no positive declaration of cause and effect. Be cautious in your claims.

■ Narration

Telling a story, like telling a good joke, is hard to do. You narrate, or tell a story, in a piece of expository writing in order to bring your argument to life.

To be effective, the narrative you use in an essay should contain carefully selected, telling details — enough to be vivid, not so many that it is boring. The narrative must be well timed: it should draw your reader into the writing or graphically illustrate a point you are making. It should hold the reader's attention: do not expand the story endlessly with "and then . . . and then . . . and then."

Use narration sparingly in essay writing. Most commonly you will find it used to relate case studies, brief anecdotes, and extended examples.

Example

> *The Bible contains many stories of dreams used as prophecies. Perhaps the most famous is the story of the dreams of the Pharoah of Egypt. He dreamed of seven fat cattle, followed by seven lean cattle, which devoured the first. Then he dreamed of seven good stalks of corn, which were destroyed by seven lean stalks of corn. These dreams Joseph interpreted as prophecies about the fate of Egypt. First, it would experience seven years of plenty, then seven years of famine. In response to Joseph's interpretation, the Pharoah stored enough food from the seven good years to protect the country from starvation during the famine that followed.[9] Such treatments of dreams as prophecy are part of many religions and illustrate the captivating power of the dream on the human imagination.*

This paragraph retells a familiar biblical story to make a point about the imaginative appeal of dreams.

The superscript numerals used throughout the sample paragraphs indicate places where a writer would have to acknowledge sources. In this case, traditional note numbers have been used. For more information on the subject of citation of sources, see Chapters 9 and 16.

■ Tips on Choosing the Right Pattern

Your choice of pattern may depend to some extent on your subject. In English, for example, one of the most common patterns is *Comparison/Contrast*. In Political Science and Sociology, you may find yourself most often choosing *Definition* or *Classification*. History makes most use of the *Cause/Effect* pattern. The most common pattern in all writing is *Example*. Choose your pattern wisely; keep its relevance to the overall thesis statement always in mind.

EXERCISES

1. Develop the following thesis statements by using at least two appropriate patterns of argument:

   a. The state of the environment demands our immediate attention.
   b. The requirements for college and university admission need to be reassessed.
   c. Nationalism needs to be replaced by global consciousness.
   d. The mass media interfere with individual privacy.
   e. Let the buyer beware!

2. Develop a thesis statement for one of the following topics:
   a. Canada's relation to America
   b. the advantages or disadvantages of technology
   For the topic chosen, develop a short introductory paragraph ending with the thesis statement. Go through the patterns of argument listed, and decide which methods would be most appropriate for developing your thesis statement. Then, outline the essay.

3. Analyze the patterns of argument in a paper you have written in the past. What are your most common patterns? What patterns could be used more effectively?

4. Analyze the patterns of argument you find in an article selected from a journal or popular magazine. List any techniques you find that you could emulate in your own work.

PART THREE

Drafting the Essay

Shaping the Essay

> You must jot down ideas as they occur to you. The jotting is simplicity itself—it is the occurring which is difficult.
>
> *Stephen Leacock*

As you develop your outline from its bare structure to its fully dressed form, remember that the shape of the essay is in your hands. Though there are guidelines you can follow, the essay is not a form to be filled in. You create the form itself, by selecting what is included and what is left out.

■ The First Draft

To make the first draft of your essay easier to write, keep the following advice in mind:

Write while you think, not after

To move from outline to essay, you need to develop your thought. This development does not involve long delays and cautious planning. Writing is not the expression of thought; it is thought itself. To avoid getting tangled up in a web of confusion, or worse, procrastination, write as you think, rather than after you have thought. Putting pen to paper, even in an unpolished way, will help you overcome the terror of the blank page and will enable you to examine your thoughts more objectively later on.

Worry as you write

This may sound like odd advice in a book meant to help you compose an essay, but the worrying stage, uncomfortable though it may be, is usually productive. Worrying is thinking. Keep the essay in the back of your mind as you do other things; carry a small notebook and make a record of passing ideas.

Plan to rewrite

Don't demand perfection of your prose the first time out. Writing demands rewriting, not only to correct but to beautify as well. The need for revision does not mean that your first draft is a failure. Writers revise not only to correct errors but also to find the smoothest, the most succinct, the most elegant way to say something. Writing without revision is like getting dressed without looking in a mirror.

Allow yourself freedom to experiment

Say something. The essay is your chance to say what you want to say (within the limits of decorum!) the way you want to say it. All that is demanded in an essay assignment is that you think independently (and perhaps with a little help from source material) and write in your own words (perhaps with the occasional quoted expert). Don't allow the fear of criticism to paralyze you at the outset. In your first draft especially, write to suit yourself.

Allow yourself space to write and to make mistakes

Double or triple space. Leave wide margins. Leave one side of the page blank. Use pencil if you like. Or use coloured markers so you can see immediately what is being added or deleted.

Cut and paste, literally (or with the aid of a word processor), in order to give yourself the chance to see the complete sequence of ideas.

Develop your own methods of quick notation

As you write, include references immediately after their occurrence in the text. Generally, use the author's last name and a page number in parentheses just after the quotation or the reference in your paper. If you use the documentation suggested by the MLA or APA (see p. 136 of this volume), this notation may be all you need. If not, your notes can be amended later.

If you are using a word processor

If you are lucky enough to be able to compose your essay on a word processor, take advantage of any of its special features that will enable you to write more quickly and efficiently. Here are some guidelines:

1. Experiment. Use the speed of the word processor to allow yourself a look at various possibilities in wording and in structure.
2. Write more critically than when you write on paper. Take advantage of the freedom from drudgery offered by the processor to move paragraphs and to revise wording.
3. Learn to proofread from the screen. Better still, double-check your proofreading. Check the screen first and then make a hard copy and check it.
4. Don't expect the machine to do everything for you. Even though the mechanical aspects of the essay should be simpler on a word processor, don't fool yourself that careful writing or rigorous revision can be eliminated.
5. Use the time you save by writing on a word processor to think your topic through more carefully, to do more intensive research, and to ferret out every small error.

■ Assembling Evidence

Avoid "tunnel vision"

The success of your essay depends not only on your ability to make your case, but also on the maturity of your critical approach—your fairness, objectivity, and sensitivity to flaws in methodology (yours and others'). Don't let emotions prevent you from assessing the evidence. You may, for example, feel strongly that Canada should provide aid to Third World countries, yet when writing an essay on the subject of development aid, you will have to assess the claims that such aid leads to economic dependency. Objectivity is essential.

Interpret your findings

You cannot expect the citation of a statistic or the inclusion of a quotation to make your point. You must *interpret* the meaning of such evidence. A survey that indicates that 75% of the student population approves of aid to Third World countries does not speak for itself. In order to interpret such findings, you need to know how many people were actually surveyed, whether or not the survey involved a fair random sampling, and whether the questions that made up the survey were clear and unbiased in their wording. Only when you have taken these factors into account can you use the figure to claim, for example, that the student population is, to a large extent, willing to support Third World development.

Avoid "blind spots"

An essay demands that you take a position with regard to the evidence you uncover. That position must, however, be based on an objective and unbiased reading of the facts. To ensure that you do not wilfully (or otherwise) misread your evidence, try to formulate both the case for and the case against your position. Include in your essay not only a defence of your thesis, but also arguments that have led you to reject contrary interpretations. For example, if you are arguing that development aid to Third World countries is a humanitarian obligation, you must consider the charge that the resulting private foreign investment is exploitative. You may find that you must concede some points. Such qualification makes your argument all the more objective in its evaluation of the data.

Aim at a better, not an ultimate, theory

When you use evidence to defend your thesis, be realistic in your goals. Your research and your thought together have led you to understand the data in a certain way. Your task is to show that your reading of the material exhibits common sense and attention to recent data. Your theory about the meaning of the evidence should help to explain something. You may find, for instance, that economic dependency only partly explains the continuing problems in the Third World and that internal, national factors play a part as well. Your theory won't be perfect—just the most reliable interpretation of the facts you have found.

■ The Conventional Shape of the Essay

In order to control your material, you must strive to achieve unity within your essay. An essay's unity is the wholeness of the vision, the focus that holds the disparate parts together. Without such wholeness, your essay will seem incomplete or rambling.

To do justice to your assembled arguments and support, the shape of your essay should meet certain of its readers' expectations. To make a good first impression on the reader, your essay should include these basic elements:

1. an *introduction*, moving from general topic to specific thesis, perhaps including a preview of its content;
2. a *body*, developing in turn each of the main points used to support your thesis statement;
3. a *conclusion*, reinforcing and/or summarizing what has been the focus of the essay and suggesting further implications.

Observing these conventional forms will ensure that your essay is clear, pointed, and emphatic from beginning to end.

A good essay possesses a sharp, comprehensive introduction and conclusion, with an expansive body that develops and supports the thesis.

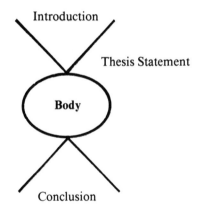

■ Maintaining Unity in the Essay

An essay is a unit: a discussion centred on one basic point. Remember that your essay should focus on your thesis statement. An essay meant to grapple with the causes of the War of 1812 should not discuss its aftermath, just as an essay treating the issue of free will in *Paradise Lost* should find no place for a discussion of epic conventions.

To keep your essay unified:

1. Keep your purpose and basic pattern of argument firmly in mind.
2. Avoid digressions, however interesting, if they cannot be connected to the thesis statement.
3. Avoid padding for the sake of word length. Instead, develop your ideas by referring to Chapter 4, on patterns of argument, and relating them to your proposed thesis statement.
4. Redesign your thesis statement (within the limits of the assignment, of course), if you find your initial focus unappealing or too limited in scope.

Above all, remember the principle of unity:

Everything in an essay should relate directly to the main focus of the paper.

EXERCISE

Read over an essay you wrote recently and note every time you digressed from the main focus of the essay and every time you added "padding."

Making an Introduction

> There's no rule on how it is to write. Sometimes it comes easily and perfectly. Sometimes it is like drilling rock and then blasting it out with charges.
>
> *Ernest Hemingway*

Think of your essay, for a moment, as if it were a person. Since an essay will establish some kind of relationship with its readers, the analogy is not altogether far-fetched. Here is some advice on how to proceed after you say "hello."

■ Strike Up a Conversation

Obviously, writing a formal essay is more complicated than starting a conversation. But the analogy should provide you with a place to start. How should you begin a conversation? One way is to startle your listener by presenting an exciting piece of information, as a preview of coming attractions. Or, as a recommendation of the value of the work you have done, you can report the words of a well-known, respected authority in relation to your topic. Another method is to pick a fight, by stating the claims, or defining the terms, of the accepted position and then challenging them. Remember that your first task is to convince your audience to pay heed to what you are saying. What all of these tactics have in common is their ability to provoke a response.

Human judgment being the superficial, lazy thing is sometimes is (and professors are by no means exempt), an essay must overcome certain prejudices about its nature. In order to present itself proudly to an instructor, an essay must show immediate signs that it will not be boring, vague, pretentious, or long-winded.

■ Write with Control

Perhaps the most common pitfall among essay writers in establishing the basis of their arguments is long-windedness. Remember that an introduction should be no longer than about one-fifth of the entire essay's length (the best introductions are short and comprehensive—don't go on). If you find that your introduction demands more space than that, you have not narrowed your topic down to a manageable size, or you should be writing a book instead! Never promise in the introduction more than you can deliver in the paper. The first few lines are the best place to limit the scope of your discussion and state the qualifications of your theories. Maintain control of your material, and have some consideration (if not some pity) on your poor beleaguered reader.

■ Write with Conviction

To avoid accusations of boredom, make sure that the introduction shows *how* what you have written matters—to you and to anyone concerned with the subject. Convincing readers that a topic is important is not simply a matter of telling them so; you have to show them, by the tone of your writing, that you are deeply engaged with the topic. Write with conviction, with the feeling that what you are saying will make a difference. Don't negate its value by suggesting that the essay's position is only your opinion. Approach the essay as if it were one side of a lively conversation. Because there is some distance between writer and reader, this interchange is not as immediate as that of conversation, but remember that there is a reader "at the other end of the line." Imagine your reader's responses as you introduce your material, just as you imagine your friend's face as she answers the telephone.

■ Be Conversant with Your Subject

Your introduction is meant to foster an existing knowledge and interest on the part of the reader. Don't tell the reader what he or she already knows. In the case of a literary essay, for example, there is no need to provide a plot summary. Any reader of such an essay should have that material well in hand. In other disciplines, this advice means avoiding the mere recital of material discussed in class, or the careful delineation of a definition that is neither contentious nor germane to what will follow. Write to communicate.

To avoid sounding pretentious, you must use your own voice and your sense of what is appropriate to the occasion. In the introduction, you must lead the reader into your way of thinking. The introduction must make both you and your reader comfortable. To get comfortable with a topic that, three weeks ago, may have been completely unfamiliar to you is part of the task of essay writing. Only when you can *talk* knowledgeably about the subject of your paper are you ready to write about it.

■ Communicate with Your Reader

If carefully designed, your introduction should tell the reader some essential things about you and your work: that you sincerely wish to communicate;

that you are conversant with your subject and have convictions about it; that you are confident, in control, and considerate of your reader. All these nouns beginning with "con" or "com" suggest the necessity of forming a relationship *with* someone or something. An introduction with these attributes demands attention and commands respect.

■ Ice-Breaking: Tactics for Opening the Essay

If you are at a loss for words when writing your introduction, try one of the strategies in the following list. Suppose, for example, that your essay topic is "Man-made health hazards in the environment."

1. Take the straight and narrow path.

State your thesis bluntly and without preamble. Follow it with a brief statement of the steps in your argument.

Example

> *It is our fundamental human right to live in a healthy environment. For this to happen, we must protect the environment from man-made health hazards.*

2. Try shock treatment.

Give your reader a striking, perhaps shocking example, statistic, or statement to get him or her interested in reading further.

Example

> *One-year-old Diane Fowler woke up in the middle of the night in the midst of a convulsion. Her temperature was dangerously high. She was rushed to the Hospital for Sick Children in Toronto, where she was diagnosed as suffering from lead poisoning. Soon after, five more members of Diane's family were diagnosed as having lead poisoning. Within two years, a large group of citizens, all living near the Toronto-based lead plant, were found to have elevated levels of lead in their blood.*

3. Engage your reader.

Remind the reader that the subject under discussion matters to him or her by showing its general importance, before you settle down to your specific line of argument.

Example

> *While some people think that environmental health hazards affect only those who work in risky occupations or who live in certain neighbourhoods, it is clear that the problem is more widespread than that. Everyone's life is endangered. Lead, for example, is in the water we drink, the air we breathe, and the food we eat. For Canadians, the likelihood of exposure to serious environmental hazard is now 100%, and even low-level exposure to substances like lead can cause serious health problems.*

EXERCISES

1. Write introductory paragraphs (complete with thesis statements) on the following topics:

   a. football
   b. shopping
   c. dreaming
   d. a social problem
   e. a matter of life and death

2. Analyze the opening paragraph or so of one of your essays. What introductory techniques are used there? Try rewriting the opening to make it stronger.

3. Find several articles in a journal related to your area of study. Analyze how these articles have introduced their subjects.

4. Read the following student paragraphs, all of which served as introductions to essays. Analyze the techniques by which they arouse the reader's interest:

   a. Baseball is a terrific game! I can watch it and peruse its statistics for hours. Unfortunately, many people do not feel the same way I do. They think baseball is a long, tedious game full of irrelevant statistics, such as Bobby Gillespie hitting .235 against left-handed pitchers in Sunday-afternoon games; however, there is much more to baseball than is initially perceived.

   b. One of the highlights of visiting Canada's capital city, Ottawa, is attending a meeting of the House of Commons. There the representatives of the people gather to debate, formally and diplomatically, how the country should be governed. The members of parliament are supposedly among the wisest in the land. Indeed, they are respected by all, with the exception of those who have seen them in the House of Commons. Those who have witnessed the leaders of our country at work might compare the Commons to a dog kennel.

   c. Earle Birney views the city from a mountain top, T.S. Eliot from the level of the street. There is a world of difference in the manner with which each poet treats his subject, yet both are concerned with the city as a reflection of the soul of man. Birney, in "Vancouver Lights," and Eliot, in "Preludes," use the city as a means of exploring the nature of man.

   d. If a ball bearing is caught between two opposing and equally powerful magnets, the tension produced by the forces of attraction and repulsion will hold it firmly in the middle, paralyzing it and rendering it motionless and unable to move in either direction. Some individuals are caught in unfulfilling relationships like the suspended ball bearing. They experience conflicting emotions, wanting to leave and at the same time wanting to stay, wanting to make choices for growth, but fearing to take risks. The push-pull force is exerting a supreme effort to keep them inert and powerless. This inertia, this paralysis, is ambivalence. Ambivalence is a powerful force that can keep individuals from making rational decisions.

Drawing a Conclusion

> When you're ready to stop, stop. If you have presented all the facts and made the point that you want to make, look for the nearest exit.
> *William Zinsser*

Your concluding paragraph is not only your last word on the subject but also an opportunity for you to reinforce your argument. Listed below are four techniques by which you may reinforce your argument in order to end your paper strongly and convincingly. The essay that builds toward a powerful conclusion will not fade out but will reverberate in the reader's mind.

■ Retrace Your Line of Thought

Retracing does not mean repeating. Since both you and the reader know where you have been, all you need to provide in your conclusion is a reminder of the steps of the journey. You need only to mention key words that have gathered meaning as the argument has proceeded in order for the astute reader (the one for whom you have been writing all along) to "catch your drift." Echo for effect, rather than for reiteration.

To remind the reader of the inherent structure of your essay, make certain to restate the thesis statement in a conclusive manner, and in different words from those that you used in the opening. Doing so will enable you to check to see if the essay has really lived up to your expectations of it. Keep in mind that the essay is meant to be a lively, though formal, conversation. A subtle reminder of the point you have made will aid the readers; a word-for-word repetition will annoy them.

■ Refocus Your Argument

Just as a film director may end a scene by changing the camera focus to wide angle or softening it, so too the essay can take a broader and less stringent view of its subject in its closing.

Widen the focus as you conclude by showing the importance of your topic beyond the immediate concerns of your paper. Beware, however, of writing an overblown conclusion such as "Milton is the world's greatest poet." Instead, include a suggestion for change or perhaps a solution to the problem you have so carefully outlined in the core of the essay.

■ Encourage Response

While the body of your essay requires you to provide answers and to be clear and definite in your thinking and wording, there is *some* room in the conclusion for you to mention tentative ideas, to pose questions, or to offer challenges to the reader. You shouldn't open the floodgates too widely, but it is a good tactic to provoke a response in your reader, provided it is relevant to the topic in question. Beware, though, of starting something you cannot finish, or of introducing a topic that sounds suspiciously like what your essay should have been about.

■ Make Your Words Resound

By the time you reach your conclusion, you should feel that no important argument for your thesis statement has been neglected. This attitude of confidence will allow you to end your paper with a bang rather than a whimper (to invoke, or rather invert, the words of T.S. Eliot). Make sure that the tone conveys a sense of finality, a sense that you have done all that can be expected within the precise bounds of your thesis statement. The conclusion should not, of course, make grand claims that your essay cannot substantiate.

■ Drawing to a Close: Tactics for Ending the Essay

When you come to the end of your essay, consider one of the following ways of formulating a conclusion. Suppose, for instance, that your paper is about the dangers of pollution:

1. Decide that enough is enough.

If you find you have nothing pressing to add, say nothing. Make sure, however, that your argument ends on a strong note. Don't stop writing just because you are tired, though.

Example

> There is nothing that we do, nothing that we eat or breathe, that does not contribute to the state of our planet, and therefore to environmentalism.

2. Take the wider view.

Examine some of the broader implications of your thesis and the questions it may have raised.

Example

> As you read through this paper, you probably thought of some things you can do to make your contribution to the preservation of the environment. Although some of these solutions may involve giving up a few of your comforts, you have probably realized that we can no longer blame the other fellow and do nothing ourselves. The poverty, pollution, and poisoning were caused by all of us and can be eliminated only with everyone's co-operation.

3. Reinforce your claim.

Remind the reader gently of your line of thought and reiterate your thesis in a slightly different form.

Example

We are all affected by pollution, but just as we are part of the problem, so we can be part of the solution. Remember these guidelines: reduce, reuse, recycle, and rebel. Reduce the use of electricity and fuel. Reuse things, rather than automatically disposing of them. Recycle refillable containers made of glass, paper, and metal. And rebel by encouraging the government to back tougher legislation to protect our environment.

EXERCISES

1. Read the following conclusions, and consider the techniques they use to draw an essay to a close:

   a. Street people are often more articulate than people you may meet at parties, who can talk only about how drunk they got once, or about their promising futures. Wild drunken behaviour is only one fact of life to street people, and promising futures are only for those who want them. For every argument we give to support a comfortable, statistically normal life, a street person can reply with a story he has picked up along the way to counter our point. Perhaps if we listened more to street people, we would see the pointlessness in worrying so much, and spending so much time worrying about money, for there are people out there who get by without both.

   b. What then is the vision that each poet has of the modern city? Birney sees the city as a symbol of man's incredible creative will, which has brought forth the light of civilization from the darkness. He sees man as self-destructive, but at the same time as heroic. He feels pride in man's daring and tenacity. Eliot, on the other hand, sees the city as both a cause of, and a manifestation of, the unhappy condition of mankind. He sees man's soul as trapped in this adverse environment and unable to find the way to redemption or to give meaning and beauty to life. He sees no remedy, but he looks on with sorrow and compassion.

   c. Since giving birth can be so rife with "discomfort" and embarrassment, it is a wonder that anyone deliberately has more than one child. Fortunately for the perpetuation of mankind, human beings have poor long-term memories for detail. It is also propitious that babies hold tremendous appeal for most people. Mother Nature knew what she was doing when she gave babies eyes like Bambi's and crooked, tremulous grins guaranteed to melt the heart of the toughest character. Because of those infant attributes, parents readily erase from their minds the pain and indignity that accompanied the baby's début, and thus the species continues.

   d. The performance appraisal is a process of evaluation used to make decisions about promotion, merit pay, or perhaps even dismissal. The appraisal helps employees assess their strengths and weaknesses and assists in career planning. Performance appraisals, when used correctly, benefit both employee and employer.

2. Analyze the last paragraph of one of the sample papers used in this book (pp. 73, 85). What techniques are used to tie things together?

3. Analyze the last paragraph or so of one of your previous essays. What techniques did you use to conclude? Can you rewrite these paragraphs to make them more effective?

4. Analyze the last paragraph of an article you find in a journal related to one of your subject areas. How does it reinforce the rest of the article?

Writing Paragraphs

Writing and rewriting are a constant search for
what it is one is saying.

John Updike

Though an essay may not be, strictly speaking, a work of art, it does offer infinite opportunities for the artistic development of your material. What follows are some suggestions on how to develop your paragraphs and how to check to see that paragraphing in the final paper is unified and coherent.

A paragraph must be about one thing. This principle of unity should be so clear that you could compose a heading for each paragraph if the assignment demanded it (and some may).

Logical connections within each paragraph must also be clear. Leaps in logic or unstated assumptions are flaws in your argument that will affect the coherence of the final paper and lose your reader's good will.

Each paragraph is a small step in your total argument, meant to lead the reader onward through your thought process. Hence, each small part must contribute to the whole pattern. Remember that each small section of your argument, each paragraph, is in fact a miniature model of the essay structure itself.

Each paragraph, like the larger essay, should contain the following elements:

1. a topic sentence that reveals the controlling idea, or thesis
2. support related to the topic sentence
3. unity of focus
4. a smooth transition to the next paragraph

■ The Topic Sentence

A typical paragraph in an essay begins with a topic sentence, a general "umbrella" statement that explains what the rest of the paragraph is about. Anything that does not relate to this controlling idea should be left out. Sometimes, writers feel that it is unprofessional to make the topic sentence too obvious, but despite their fears, a clear topic sentence is an asset. Because the essay is, by its nature, rather repetitive in structure, you may be simply repeating, in different words, a point that you previewed in your thesis statement. For instance, your thesis statement may be that triage is an essential, if difficult, part of a good health-care system because it enables medical teams to decide which patients must be attended to first. In your first paragraph you have defined the term "triage." In the second paragraph, you might begin by stating that one of the criteria for setting priorities for care is the patient's chance of survival. Your next paragraph might begin with a topic sentence that mentions the next criterion: the patient's ability to wait. Each of these criteria would be developed in turn.

A topic sentence need not necessarily begin your paragraphs, but for less experienced writers, and in essay writing generally, it usually does.

■ The Support

Your support may take several forms:

1. examples
2. statistics
3. connected reasons/definitions
4. authorities

Approach the undeveloped arguments in your outline with these four categories in mind. The sources of support will depend on the nature of the assignment: a formal research essay may require all four; a less formal paper will rely chiefly on reasons and examples for its strength.

■ Developing Support for Your Paragraphs

Remember, as you weave your outline into paragraphs, that each discrete unit must ultimately contribute something to the illustration of the essay's thesis statement. The paragraphs argue in its defence or show its validity.

Some of the following methods are formal adaptations of techniques of argument you may have used before. The list is by no means complete; try to think of other equally effective battle plans.

Present the facts of the case

These facts may include statistics used to prove your point. Don't take it for granted that your readers know what you know about the subject.

Example

> *Frozen dinners, according to their manufacturers, are steadily increasing in popularity, perhaps because of the widespread use of microwave ovens and because of the pace of modern society. Indeed, according to one producer of these goods, over 80% of households buy these products on a regular basis. One wonders, however, how anyone can bear to eat them.*

Show and tell

To keep the line of thought going, remember that it is always best to argue by example, rather than by precept. Don't just tell your readers about something. Show them, wherever possible, how your idea works by giving an example.

Example

Lumped in one plastic partition of the frozen dinner is a white, viscous mound with a substance faintly resembling butter sliding greasily down its pasty sides. Its likeness on the box wrapper indicates the presence of potatoes in that location, but the taste is reminiscent of the last stamp you licked. The texture is perennially similar across all brands of frozen dinners—that of wet plaster. Incredibly, manufacturers of frozen dinners even get their potatoes to taste like wet plaster, an unfortunate consistency, if you will excuse the pun.

Establish connections

Find something in the point you are making that relates to your own experience or to that of your readers. If the essay is formal rather than informal in tone, adapt this advice to show the readers why the subject is important to them.

Example

Hope springs eternal as the harried consumer tries different brands of frozen dinners. The diabolically clever chemists must do free-lance work for all the major manufacturers because Brand A's "Chicken Marengo" tastes disconcertingly like Brand X's "He-Man Beef Platter." You may wonder how they do it. A better question may be "Why do we let them?" The answer is probably that fast food, despite its drawbacks, is ubiquitous and unavoidable in a society in which no one has time to cook.

Define your terms

If the terminology is clear, don't bother telling your readers what they already know. If, on the other hand, you think that a closer look at a word or phrase that is part of your topic will help your case, draw their attention to it.

Example

Although frozen dinners claim to be made of frozen food, the claim is debatable. Take, for example, what passes for dessert in one of these trays. Gustatory delight is expected because of a tantalizing picture on the box and an imaginative description— spiced apple supreme, for instance. Alas, the unsuspecting fruit has met a fate similar to that of the potatoes. Magnificent, tart, crunchy McIntosh apples have been reduced to apple-facsimile chunks, improved by the thoughtful addition of a charming artificial flavour mixed in with a gelatinous goo. When the fruit is eaten, the fleshy texture is so odd that, except for the absence of pain, the consumer cannot be sure he has not bitten his tongue and is happily chewing on it.

Call in an expert

Convince your reader by turning to an expert for support. Don't expect readers to take your word for something, if the words of a specialist in the area are available to buttress your own. If the person to whom you refer is a respected authority, your argument will be enriched by his or her utterance.

Example

The sad truth is that diners everywhere exist on frozen food because no one has time any more for home cooking. While we all still have to eat, none of us is eager to prepare dinner—for ourselves or for others. Because time is precious, and frozen food is ubiquitous, we do not rebel against the horrors of monosodium glutamate, salt, and artificial colouring. As Shirley Conran says, "Life is too short to stuff a mushroom."

Note that the source of this quotation would have to be acknowledged, using some consistent form of documentation—a subject covered in detail in Chapter 16.

■ Unity

A paragraph, like the essay itself, should have demonstrated the development of your thought by the time your reader finishes it. Each paragraph should lead the reader along in a logical and coherent manner. If your outline has been well planned, the progress of your thinking should be orderly, and your conclusion clear. Your paragraphs should each form a discrete unit, and each paragraph should be clearly connected to what precedes and to what follows.

Example

It is interesting that beets are rarely offered in these frozen dinner simulations. Possibly that is because beets stubbornly insist on having a beet-like tang no matter how they are diced, sauced, or otherwise adulterated. Such a renegade authentic flavour might take the targeted "average consumer" by surprise. He or she might then realize that the other items on the slab are pale imitations of the real thing. Since that realization could have dire consequences for the manufacturer's cash flow, only co-operative vegetables grace the microwaveable plastic tray.

In this example, the author discusses the quality of vegetables normally used in frozen dinners, by pointing out one variety that never appears. The paragraph then goes on to offer a theory for the beet's conspicuous absence, one that connects this paragraph to the overall notion of the lack of flavour found in frozen dinners.

■ Pinning the Pieces Together—Transitions

Despite the basic structural independence of the paragraph, the reader must be able to appreciate how it fits into the whole essay. To make the connections clear to the reader, an essayist must use appropriate transitions and linking devices.

Transitions are signals of a turn in thought. They often pose a problem for the novice essay writer simply because our methods of changing or developing the subject in conversation are much less formal and much more spontaneous than in written, rhetorical form.

Ask yourself what your favourite techniques of transition in speech are. Then try to categorize the situations that prompt you to use them. You may find that your list of transitions includes such statements as: "And you know what else?" to add to or elaborate on a point: "You see," to explain in greater detail; "Sure, but," to disagree with another's argument, at the same time conceding to some degree; "What if . . .?" to put forward an hypothesis; "Anyhow," to dismiss the view of your interlocutor; or "As I said before, to reinforce an earlier point.

Many of these transitions cannot be easily transferred to the printed page. They are too casual to suit the public occasion of the essay. In their stead, the writer must become familiar with and use more formal transitions to enhance the power of his or her rhetoric.

Transitions have many uses. Here are some examples of various transitions:

TO ADD	**TO ENUMERATE**
and	first, second,
also	first, next, last
in addition	
furthermore	
as well	
TO ILLUSTRATE	**TO SUMMARIZE**
for example	to conclude
for instance	in short
in other words	finally
that is	
TO QUALIFY	**TO DRAW A CONCLUSION**
often	hence
generally	therefore
specifically	as a result
usually	consequently
TO CHANGE DIRECTION	**TO ESTABLISH CAUSE**
but	because
however	for
conversely	
although	
whereas	

Good transitions are like carefully sewn seams. Although not readily noticeable, they are the means by which the garment is held together. Shoddy workmanship in your transitions may cause your essay to fall apart—an embarrassing state for something that is appearing in print and is being presented to someone you wish to impress.

■ Checking the Overall Pattern of Your Paragraphs

There are two basic tests for the aesthetic appeal of the paragraph.

One of these is to read the first sentence of each paragraph to check if the line of thought is clearly maintained throughout the entire work. That is, do the sentences themselves act as subheadings to guide the reader through your design? (*Note*: This test assumes that most paragraphs begin with a topic sentence. Sometimes, however, the topic sentence may appear at the end.)

Another test of effective paragraphing involves looking at the length of the paragraphs themselves on the printed page. Is each of them a manageable length? Most paragraphs will have at least three sentences: a topic sentence introducing the theme that follows, some kind of support, and some elaboration of that support. This is a guideline only; occasionally, a one- or two-sentence paragraph is used for effect. Usually, though, it is a sign of poor thought development and insufficient support.

The layout counts too. Break your paragraphs with an eye to avoiding a "choppy" page or one that presents a daunting block of type.

EXERCISES

1. Develop a paragraph, using your definition of a term. Compare it with the definition you find in the dictionary as a starting point. Try one of these words:

   romance   embarrassment
   failure   boredom

2. Develop a paragraph using a statistic or a quoted authority as support. Look through newspapers or weekly magazines for possible topics, or try these:

   men and women   fame
   acting   friendship
   old age   religion

3. Write a paragraph establishing a connection or comparison. Develop your own comparison, or try one of the following:

   boys vs. men   girls vs. women
   workers vs. loafers   diplomacy vs. hypocrisy

4. Develop two paragraphs: one using a real example and one using a hypothetical example. Find your real example in the newspaper, and make up another on the same subject. Try one of these subjects:

   someone who wins the lottery
   someone who narrowly escapes an accident
   someone with a particular health condition

5. Write two paragraphs: one using a series of small examples to make the same point and one using an extended example to support the same point. Pick any one of these:

   how to find love
   how to make friends
   how to deal with enemies
   how to get a job

6. Analyze the structure of the following paragraphs. How is unity achieved? What logical connectives or transitions are used?

   a. Canada has been experiencing rapidly increasing technical efficiency. We, as a population, are reaping the benefits of receiving more and more output from our productive efforts. But do the benefits of better technical efficiency outweigh the cost of increasing numbers of unemployed? The answer is no.

In addition to increased technical efficiency, there has been an upswing in the degree of automation within industry. Machinery is replacing the vast quantity of manpower once used by the great corporations of the nation. As well, we have increased the amount of trade with foreign nations, many of which have a comparative advantage in the production of certain goods. Today our balance of trade indicates that our exports outweigh our imports. Anyone who cares to tally the number of imported cars and the number of domestically manufactured cars will testify that the import car companies are steadily increasing their share of the Canadian automobile market; as a result, the demand for Canadian labour has decreased.

b. The best way to cope with airports is to follow some basic steps. When you arrive at the airport prior to your journey, make sure that you enter the Departures Terminal and not the Arrivals Terminal, or else you could find yourself missing your plane. Once inside the proper terminal, find a porter to carry your luggage for you, locate the desk of your airline, and join the appropriate line for checking-in procedures. The desk personnel will take your luggage and place it on a scale to be weighed. They will then tag your luggage and place the bags on a conveyer belt, where they will be taken to another area to be sorted and put on the plane.

Once your luggage has been cleared, your purse or any other small bags will be tagged as cabin luggage and returned to you. The desk clerk will then ask you for your preference in seating. You have a choice of seats by a window, by an aisle, or in the middle of the row. Having confirmed your seat, the clerk writes the appropriate number on your ticket, and you then try to find the number of the departure gate for your flight.

Most airports have monitors that will inform you of your gate and terminal number. Locate your flight number on the screen, and scan across to the listings of gate numbers and departure times. This task is not difficult, but if you have any problems, ask someone near you for help. Together you should be able to solve the puzzle with ease.

Shortly before you are scheduled to leave, you will be called into your departure lounge. As you enter the gate leading to the lounge, you will be required to go through security measures. Each person must place his or her cabin luggage on a small conveyer belt that passes through an x-ray machine. The machine scans the luggage for any metal objects that may be packed inside the cases. You will also be required to pass through a scanning device that detects any metallic objects hidden in your clothing. After receiving clearance, you collect your belongings and enter the lounge.

As you board the plane, a flight attendant will check your ticket and direct you to your seat. There are also other attendants available for help if you need it. Before takeoff, someone will instruct you on some essential safety precautions, and finally, you will be left to enjoy your flight.

7. Select paragraphs from essays you wrote in the past. Rewrite any that seem to you to lack a clear topic sentence, unity, or smooth transitions.

8. Find an article in a journal or magazine that is of interest to you. Check to see what transitions are used throughout the piece.

Paraphrasing Sources and Integrating Quotations

> Quotation: The art of repeating erroneously the words of another.
>
> *Ambrose Bierce*

Not all essays will demand that you use sources other than your own imagination and general knowledge of the world. Many essays, however, will include, as part of the requirements, a knowledge of background sources, all of which must be acknowledged to avoid charges of plagiarism.

Source material, while often a significant part of the essay, does not speak for itself. Remember that the function of paraphrased and quoted matter is to provide support for your arguments. You are responsible for the use you make of the source material. Not only must you be accurate in your representation of it, but you also must be prepared to use it thoughtfully to support your viewpoint.

When you find an idea or a quotation in another source, you are obliged to inform your reader of its origins, even if it is an idea that you already had yourself. Except for the classroom, which is usually considered common domain, the sources of your ideas must be listed in your papers. If you are in doubt about whether or not to include a source for some particular information, put yourself in the reader's place. Would he or she ask, "How do you know this is true?" If so, you need to mention the source.

Quotations and paraphrase are used as support in rather different ways. Quotations are most often used in an essay dealing with literature or a book review, where the main trustworthy source of information is the text of a work itself.

Paraphrase, on the other hand, is used when the exact words are not as important, but the facts they present are; hence, paraphrase is the most common method of using source material in the social sciences. If you find that you must refer to a theory or to an explanation of the meaning of some data, the best plan is to paraphrase. Remember, as you take notes, to paraphrase rather than to quote, taking special care with statistics and their implications.

When you paraphrase some part of a book or article for inclusion as support in your essay, try to get at its meaning. Try to rephrase the thought as if you were teaching the material to someone. Make notes with this principle in mind, taking care to "boil down" the facts and reduce them to their simplest terms, without distorting them. Focus on the thesis statement, topic sentences, and key words, and don't let yourself get bogged down in details. Think the words through rather than just copying them.

Both quotations and paraphrase are used to support your arguments. When you select material from sources, consider the use you intend to make of it. None of the sources will speak for itself; you must demonstrate how a source relates to the case you are building. For this reason, you should usually introduce source material and comment on its function in your paper, rather than assuming the reader will make the necessary connections.

■ Borrow Only What You Need

Borrow words, phrases, and sentences only if they add something essential that you do not already possess. Among these essentials are **credibility, power, and eloquence.**

The quotations that follow are taken from Michael Hornyansky's brilliant essay, "Is Your English Destroying Your Image?" *In the Name of Language!*, ed. Joseph Gold (Toronto: Macmillan, 1975)

Credibility

Quote to improve credibility by citing a respected and recognized authority. Or use the quotation as a target for attack, to illustrate that the source itself is doubtful and the object of your critical scrutiny.

Example

> The CBC's news-readers, once modestly reliable (meaning they could be counted on to apologize for errors) have lost their supervisor of broadcast language and now commit cheerfully such barbarisms as "It sounds like he's going to reform."

Power

Quote to demonstrate the power you have at your fingertips, but only to the extent that you will use the quotation. A carefully integrated quotation will show the reader that you have made yourself at home with the sources you have used. Your work will then illustrate your power to cut through trivial details to find the point that demands attention.

Example

> Not all change is progress. Some of it has to be resisted, and when possible reversed. If the last ditch needs defending, I'll take my place alongside Samuel Johnson:
>
>> If the changes we fear be thus irresistible, what remains but to acquiesce with silence, as in the other insurmountable distresses of humanity? It remains that we retard what we cannot repel, that we palliate what we cannot cure.
>>
>> (Preface to the Dictionary)

Eloquence

Quote rather than paraphrase when no rewording could ever hope to recapture the obvious eloquence of the original writer. Bear in mind that these instances are rare.

Example
***

As Samuel Johnson observes, "languages are the pedigree of nations."

■ Begging, Borrowing, and Stealing

In order to avoid accusations of theft, a writer, when quoting, must acknowledge a debt to a source. Don't interpret this to mean that you must quote whenever you borrow. When you paraphrase or when you make reference to an idea, you will also admit your indebtedness. Quote only when it is rhetorically the best tactic: that is, when it adds credibility, power, or eloquence.

Technically, you have not stolen an idea as long as you document its original occurrence. Failure to acknowledge a source is illegitimate borrowing, or plagiarism.

Legitimate borrowing takes place when a writer makes sparing use of some source material by fitting it carefully in the body of his or her essay, without altering it or distorting it in a way that would upset the author.

Avoid borrowing quotations in such a way that the original meaning is changed or even contradicted. The classic example of this shifty tactic is the movie review cited in an advertisement. It may read, for example, "stunning . . . amazing . . . not to be believed," when what the reviewer really said was, "A work stunning in its ignorance, amazing in its clumsy handling of the script, and not to be believed when its advertising describes it as the movie of the year."

■ The Fit, Form, and Function of Quotations

The quoted material must fit. It must relate directly to the point under discussion, and it must say something significant. Although quoting often seems like a form of pedantic name-dropping, that is not its rightful purpose.

The function of the quotation is usually to illustrate a point that you have already made in your own words. Bringing in an authority on the subject does not, after all, prove anything; it simply shows your awareness of the position of the experts, whether they be on your side or against you.

The form of the quotation is often the most difficult part of essay writing for the novice. Wherever possible, weave borrowed material unobtrusively into the body of your paper, rather than simply tacking it on.

Tacking quotations on

While it may be a relief to stop writing and turn over the responsibility for illustrating your thesis to an authority, proceed with caution. Stopping in the midst of a sentence to introduce someone else (usually with a grand and unnecessary flourish) will diminish your own authority as writer.

When you quote, you must remain on the scene, controlling the situation, rather than giving the floor to someone else. Remember, at all times, that the essay is *your* work. When you quote, do not withdraw completely as if another speaker has been hired to do the job for you.

If you have been in the habit of employing long quotations from your source material, try this experiment with one of your past essays. Read the material through quickly. Do you find yourself skimming over the quoted material, or worse, skipping it altogether? Imagine what effect this kind of reading will have on an essay that depends heavily on outside authorities to make its case.

Weaving quotations in

Wherever possible, make quoted material part of your own sentence structure. This tactic is more difficult but worth the extra effort. First, it will ensure that your reader cannot so easily skip those sections of the paper. Second, it will probably force you to cut quoted material down to the bare essentials, to look at it more closely, and to think of its direct relation to your own thought.

Example

> When a mechanic reports that "she's runnin' real good," it takes a pretty stuffy professor to reply that "it is running rather well."

To make this technique work to its fullest advantage, there are some rules to keep in mind.

1. Use an ellipsis (. . .) to indicate words that have been left out. But never use ellipses in a way that misrepresents the original. Ellipses are permissible only when you are making cosmetic changes (such as omitting a connective structure that would not make sense out of context). Keep in mind that you do *not* need ellipses at the start of a quotation, even if you did not include the beginning of a sentence in what you quoted, and remember that four dots are used when the omitted words come between two sentences. In other cases, only three dots are necessary.

Example

> Hornyansky comments that "in our democratic, colloquial society you are more likely to be censured for using no slang. . . . But of course there are risks in using it too. . . . argot that suits one milieu may draw sneers in another."

The original reads as follows:

> I would repeat that in our democratic, colloquial society you are more likely to be censured for using no slang at all. But of course there are risks in using it too. Some sober groups may find your flip ways unacceptable; argot that suits one milieu may draw sneers in another.

2. Use square brackets (even if you have to add them in black pen) to indicate words that you have added. Usually you will need these only to indicate small cosmetic changes (such as changing a pronoun to a noun

or changing a verb tense to make it consistent with the rest of the verbs in your sentence). Occasionally, you may need square brackets to add a word or two to clarify the context of the quotation.

Example

Hornyansky addresses "third- and fourth-generation Canadians who . . . [speak] English (sort of, you know?)."

The original reads as follows:

For I teach third- and fourth-generation Canadians who have spoken English (sort of, you know?) since the crib, yet who have no more sense of English idiom than a recent arrival from the Old Country.

3. When you use a complete sentence to introduce a quotation, follow it with a colon. Otherwise, use a comma or whatever punctuation you would use if the quotation marks were not there.

Example

On the subject of pretentiousness in grammar, Hornyansky remarks, "A question like 'Whom do you mean?' really deserves the answer it gets from Pogo: 'Youm, that's whom.' "

4. Make the terminal punctuation of the quoted material serve your purposes, rather than those of the original. In other words, if the quotation appears at the end of your sentence, close it with a period, even if a comma or other punctuation was used originally.

Example

The original reads as follows:

For he knows that grammar varies inversely as virility; and that if you continue on down to the stadium, you'll find that nobody there plays well.

Your paper will read this way:

Hornyansky believes "grammar varies inversely as virility."

5. Quote exactly. Do *not* distort a quotation, accidentally or deliberately. The first offence is carelessness, the second fraud. If you detect an error of spelling or grammar in the original, you may tell your reader that it is not your mistake by following it immediately with the word [sic] (in brackets as shown). This notation will tell the reader that the fault is not yours.

Example

Hornyansky cites the Hon. John Turner's advertisement "in a British newspaper that his four children require a kind and loving nannie [sic].' "

6. Use single quotation marks for a quotation within a quotation, as in the preceding example.
7. Indent passages of prose that are longer than four lines and passages of poetry longer than two lines. When you indent, quotation marks are no longer necessary.

Example

Hornyansky insists on the importance of developing one's own writing style:

> *A man at the mercy of his own style is as comic, and as much to be pitied, as a man at the mercy of drink. Your style ought to express what you are, and you are not the same person on all occasions, in every company. If you seem to be, you are a bore.*

8. When you have gone to the trouble to quote a source, use it. Explain it, remark on its significance, analyze it, do something to show what it contributes to the whole paper. Don't assume its importance is self-evident.

9. Use quotations sparingly. The essay is meant primarily to present *your* views on a given subject.

Writing the Essay

Finding Your Voice: Essay Types

> The essayist . . . can pull on any sort of shirt, be any sort of person, according to his mood or his subject matter.
>
> *E.B. White*

Role playing is a vital part of the skill of essay writing. You must write the essay confident of your role as an expert. In this chapter, we will modify the general principles of essay writing according to the various purposes of different types of essays, and describe a role you might adopt as the author of one of these types. In addition, the chapter emphasizes the kind of reader or audience that each of the different essay types has. All of the types described share the general characteristics that we have already discussed:

1. a narrow thesis statement
2. a clear outline
3. carefully delineated patterns of argument
4. a unified structure—introduction, body, and conclusion
5. a coherent approach to the integration of support materials
6. an attention to sentence structure, emphasis, and tone

Remember that many of the steps involved in writing the different types of essays described in this chapter overlap. But whether an essay is meant as an informal discussion or as a formal research paper, the steps outlined above are essential. No less important are the steps in revision described in Chapter 17.

This chapter will show you how to prepare yourself for certain specialized types of essay writing. Consult it for advice geared to the particular task at hand.

 ## The Expository Essay—Essay as Teacher

> To write simply is as difficult as to be good.
> *Somerset Maugham*

The expository essay is the most common essay assignment. It is based on the premise that you learn best about something by trying to teach it to someone else. In other words, the expository essay asks you to play the role of teacher, by presenting your chosen material according to your sense of its meaning and structure.

The expository essay exposes: it shows your approach to a particular subject. As in all essay writing, you must develop a general topic into a specific thesis statement, you must prepare an outline, and you must determine the patterns of argument appropriate to your discussion. The expository essay is different only because its object is primarily to *teach*, rather than to persuade, to present research material, to review, or to express personal conviction.

There are four stages involved in writing the expository essay:

1. Finding your focus
2. Planning your structure
3. Adjusting your level of language
4. Testing your results

These stages, while much the same as those outlined in the sections on developing, designing, and drafting the basic essay, are all affected by your role as teachers, and hence they need special consideration.

■ The Role of the Expository Essay

Before you begin, try to see your task in terms of its audience and its purpose.

AUDIENCE: a curious, but uninformed reader, whom you address in a professional but approachable way

PURPOSE: to present some important idea in a way that clarifies it, shows your attitude toward it, and answers questions the reader might have

With these criteria in mind, you can now adjust the stages in writing to suit the occasion.

Finding your focus

1. Find a subject that you know something about and are genuinely interested in, if possible.
2. Establish your objectives. Like a teacher, you should know what you want your reader to learn from your work.
3. Limit your subject to what can be thoroughly explained within the word length of the assignment. What you propose to show or explain is, in this case, your thesis statement.

Example

Subject:	*Forest-fire management*
Objective:	*To show how it is done*
Limitation:	*The step-by-step process of forest-fire management: prevention and control*

Planning your structure

1. Break down the parts of your subject clearly in an outline.
2. Choose the pattern(s) of argument that will allow you to explain most clearly.
3. Connect the steps in your thought logically and clearly.

Example

Pattern of argument: *Process: how forest fires are managed*
Breakdown of ideas: *Rough outline*
Thesis: *The Ministry of Natural Resources every year sets in motion a regular plan by which to combat forest fires that threaten to destroy Canada's natural resources.*
Body: *The Ministry does several things to control forest fires:*
1. *it establishes central locations where fire fighting begins*
2. *it predicts what areas are most endangered and maps these areas in detail*
3. *it monitors weather conditions and keeps records of soil moisture and amounts of precipitation*
4. *it monitors weather predictions*
5. *it uses aerial patrols and lightning towers to keep watch*
6. *it mobilizes fire crews when fire or smoke is reported*
7. *it dispatches water bombers and erects fire camps in crisis situations*
8. *it supplies all types of fire-fighting equipment*

Conclusion: *Fire fighting in Canada's forest regions is a careful process, dedicated to ensuring the protection of precious natural resources.*

Adjusting your level of language

1. Keep your reader's level of knowledge in mind.
2. Define all terms likely to be unfamiliar to the reader.
3. Make language concrete, concise, and clear.

Example

Level of knowledge: Provide enough background in the introduction so that the reader will know why forest-fire management is important.

> *In 1988 alone, despite preventative measures, a total of 1202 forest fires ravaged 361 319.6 hectares of prime timber.*

Use of terms: Explain terms like "water bombers" and any other terms unlikely to be familiar to a reader.

> *A water bomber is a large and cumbersome government-owned plane that can douse a fire with 5400 litres of water.*

Concrete, concise, clear language: Tell what a fire fighter does, rather than what fire management is in the abstract. Include plenty of detail.

> *Maps that show area landscapes precisely enable officers to see what sort of timber may be threatened by forest fires and what buildings, such as summer cottages and outpost camps, are in immediate or anticipated danger.*

Testing your results

1. Check your work to see that it is as clear as possible. Put yourself in your reader's place: would you learn from the essay?

2. Have someone else read your work to see that it is readily understandable.
3. Proofread carefully to see that your writing does justice to your thoughts.

■ The Persuasive Essay—Essay as Lawyer

> Why shouldn't we quarrel about a word? What is the good of words if they aren't important enough to quarrel over?
>
> *G.K. Chesterton*

The persuasive essay aims at convincing the reader of the truth and validity of your position. Its subject matter is controversial, its thesis one view of the issue. Your task is to win your reader over with your credibility, your wealth of support, and your good reasoning.

Unlike the expository essay, which simply aims to *show* the reader something, the persuasive essay, by taking one side of a controversial issue, aims to *convince* the reader.

Prepare the persuasive essay according to the following stages:

1. Study the issues
2. Pick a side—your thesis statement
3. Make a case for the defence—your support
4. Consider opposing viewpoints, and qualify or refute accordingly
5. Test your argument for fairness and effectiveness
6. Direct your argument, first in outline, then in final form

A persuasive essay may or may not demand that you engage in extensive research to support your case. It does, however, demand that you keep your writing role in mind.

■ The Role of the Persuasive Essay

Tailor your essay to fit its special demands.

AUDIENCE: readers who have not made their minds up about a controversial matter and who are willing to make a fair and impartial judgment

PURPOSE: to convince them that your informed opinion on a particular subject is the best one

With these points in mind, consider the stages of the persuasive essay. Suppose you are writing a paper on the accessibility of health care. Research is not a major requirement; what is required is your independent, well-formulated viewpoint toward this controversial subject.

Studying the issues

Before you take sides, you must examine all the angles of the question. Make a list of pros and cons about any issue that must be decided or possible answers to any question that must be settled.

Example

Issue: *Should the government continue to influence the distribution of physicians across the country in order to improve health-care access?*

PROS
— health care should be accessible to everyone
— rural areas are underserviced; most specialists are located in cities
— rural areas often lack hospital services

CONS
— doctors, particularly specialists, must be near hospitals
— the financial constraints of building and maintaining hospitals in rural areas are overwhelming
— the cost of health care itself impedes access to it

Picking a side

1. Choose the side for which you can muster the most support. If possible, choose a thesis that you genuinely believe in.
2. Define your position by making a claim or by arguing against another's claim.

Example

Side chosen: *The distribution of physicians has no real bearing on health-care access.*

Position defined: *The current distribution of physicians does not affect health-care access. The high cost of health care is the main constraint to adequate access.*
1. *Physicians, particularly specialists, must be near medical facilities to run their practices effectively.*
2. *Physicians, therefore, should not be penalized for their decision to practise in cities, as they have been in Quebec and British Columbia.*
3. *The number of physicians should not be increased, as it has been in the rest of Canada, since that "solution" only increases the cost of an expensive health-care system.*
4. *More hospitals cannot be built and maintained in rural areas without increasing expenditures even more.*
5. *The current situation, where general practitioners tend to work in towns and rural areas and specialists choose cities, is the only workable way of balancing cost and access.*

Making a case for the defence

1. Gather support for your arguments. In some instances this support will come from books or journals, though it may also come from your own clear understanding of the issue.
2. Use your own reasons, and if research is required, use statistics and expert opinion as further support. Remember to acknowledge sources.

Example

(Expert Opinion)

Accessibility is a fundamental principle of Canadian health insurance. The 1966 Medical Care Act "requires insured services to be delivered in a manner that does not impede or preclude, either directly or indirectly . . . reasonable access.''[1] In keeping with this principle, both federal and provincial governments have tried to change the geographic distribution of doctors in an effort to correct a perceived inequitable distribution of physicians. They hoped thereby to improve access to health services in rural areas.

Example

(Statistics)

In the 1960s and early 1970s, the federal government attributed the low physician-to-population ratio in rural areas to an overall shortage of doctors in the country. They believed that if there were more doctors rural areas would no longer be underserviced.[2] So, the Canadian government responded to the problem by increasing the capacity of domestic medical schools and opening immigration to physicians. Between 1968 and 1974, the number of physicians in Canada grew by 8151, or 36%;[3] however, the distribution of physicians between rural and urban areas remained disproportionate, and the gap even worsened in Ontario.[4] In fact, the growth in the number of physicians increased health-care costs, but it did not improve the accessibility of health services.

Example

(Reasons)

Actually, the increase in the number of physicians to which governmental controls has led is responsible for increasing health-care costs; to build more hospitals would increase these costs even more. Given that funds are limited, if every small town were provided with a fully equipped hospital, then the more expensive equipment and treatments—like CAT scans and cancer treatments—would not be available anywhere in Canada. It might also become necessary to impose restrictions on accessibility similar to the rationing of health care in Britain where—as a means of containing health costs—kidney dialysis is not available to National Health Service patients over fifty-five years of age.[5]

Considering opposing viewpoints

1. Anticipate objections to your arguments as you go along.
2. Treat the opposition fairly.

Example

Anticipated argument: *In spite of these arguments, the number of physicians in rural areas is still smaller than it should be to ensure access to health-care services.*

Fair treatment: *a counter-argument that analyzes the problem closely*

Although rural areas tend to have fewer physicians per capita than cities, the difference in available medical services is not necessarily proportional to the difference in the respective physician-to-population ratios. Family and general practitioners gravitate toward smaller towns, while specialists tend to settle in cities.[6] The significance of this fact lies in the kinds of medical care these doctors provide. GPs perform a considerably wider range of services than do specialists. To some degree, then, one GP acts as a substitute for the many different specialists available in the city, so access to health care may not be as unequal as the present geographic distribution of physicians implies.

Testing your argument for fairness and effectiveness

1. Check for fallacies, or flaws, in your argument.
2. Weigh your words carefully, avoiding biased or vague, unconsidered words.

When writing (or reading) any persuasive essay, you may fall prey to a number of logical errors in your thinking. Remember that certain arguments are not in the spirit of fair play. Learn to recognize the following faulty arguments or fallacies and avoid them in your own writing:

1. Accepting glib generalizations. An argument that uses catch phrases like "Canadian identity" or "freedom of the individual" in an unthinking way may just be appealing to what the words conjure up, rather than to any thoughtful meaning assigned to them by the writer. Make sure such general appeals can be pinned down to specifics. If the mayor of your city argues that he will work to increase "civic pride," ask what specifics such a general statement entails.

2. Arguing *ad hominem*. This kind of argument distracts readers from the issue being discussed and, instead, uses personal attacks against an opponent. For example, someone might argue that health-insurance fees should not go up because doctors are interested only in making money. Here the personal charge being made may have nothing to do with the issue.

3. Establishing faulty cause and effect. This kind of faulty reasoning assumes that there is a connection between two events simply because one followed the other. For instance, if a political party claims that it is responsible for a drop in interest rates that occurred during its period in office, we need to ask if such a drop might have occurred regardless. After all, there may be many other ways of explaining changes in interest rates.

4. Making a faulty analogy. Often we make analogies, or comparisons, in order to show significant similarities between things. We must, however, always take care to make sure that such comparisons are fair. Commercials are often the chief offenders in this regard. Is a day without orange juice really like a day without sunshine? Check to make sure that your own comparisons are appropriate.

5. Assuming an "either/or" situation. One of our commonest assumptions is that there are always two sides to any issue. In fact, there may be many more than two sides. See to it that you do not phrase your arguments in such a way that they falsify the problem. It is probably not true that if you don't believe in free enterprise, then you are a communist. Be aware of other possibilities between extremes.

6. Jumping on a bandwagon. When you deal with a controversial topic, make sure that you examine the issues carefully before arriving at your own point of view. To argue that something is right because it is "modern," or "current," or "up-to-date," or because everyone is in favour of it, will not stand up.

7. Begging the question. You beg the question when you assume the truth of what you are trying to prove. For example, if you argue that books should not be taxed, it is not enough to say that no one could possibly support a tax on books because it will lead to increasing illiteracy. The onus is on you to prove that illiteracy will increase; you cannot simply assume so.

Example

You may want to argue against this stated position:

Health-care access would be more equitable if physicians were more concerned with taking care of patients than with making money.

Checking for flaws: *Look at the underlying biases of the statement.*

This statement assumes that doctors practise in cities in order to make more money than they would in rural areas, but no proof is advanced for the claim. Here, in other words, the argument begs the question.

Weighing your words: *It is important to find evidence to justify any claim that you intend to make. The argument above rests on an unexamined assumption.*

Directing your argument

1. Remind your readers of the points you are making by reinforcing those points as you go along.
2. Engage your readers as comrades-in-arms, not as antagonists. Assume that they are reasonable and open-minded about the issue. Do not assume that they are antagonistic.

Example

Look at these techniques in the following paragraphs concluding the paper on access to health care:

Since every small town does not have a hospital and physicians are not located in proportion to demand, barriers to access to health services unquestionably exist; however, the cost of breaking down these barriers is higher than the cost of their presence. Ultimately, then, it is the cost of health care itself that impedes equal access. With limited government funds, equality of accessibility to health services is little more than an idealist's dream. So far, measures to make such services more accessible have invariably increased costs by more than they have improved access. Policies aimed at changing the distribution of physicians and hospitals are not the solution. Clearly, the federal and provincial governments need to change their approach to the issue of health-care access.

Reinforcement: *Summary of the line of argument*

■ The Essay Examination — Essay as Athlete

> All good writing is swimming under water and holding your breath.
>
> *F. Scott Fitzgerald*

Essay examinations are frequently a source of panic because they strip the writer down to the bare essentials. Without hours of preparation to cover your flaws, whether in knowledge or fluency, you may feel exposed—unless your work is genuinely in good shape. An essay examination, because of its time limitations, is brief but not without style.

The advice that follows will help you write a better examination, if you approach it in stages:

1. Getting in shape
2. Coping with exam shyness
3. Making the material fit
4. Taking the plunge
5. Standing out in a crowd

■ The Role of the Essay Examination

Remember your reader and your aim:

AUDIENCE: an expert (not an antagonist) who wishes to test your knowledge and facility in his or her discipline

PURPOSE: to show what you have learned and how you can apply it

Getting in shape

An examination is only the product. What determines its outcome is your preparation, not only in the nervous hours immediately before it, but in the days and weeks preceding it as well.

To make your performance on the exam less fraught and more predictable, prepare for it gradually. If you have faced your fears throughout the year, the final countdown should not be anxiety-ridden. At least, your conscience will be clear if you have attended class, read the textbooks, and completed the course work.

Coping with exam shyness

Analyze the shape you're in. Be brave. Take a good hard look at yourself. Judge your past performance in the course. Consider the amount of work you have done. If you're already in good shape, this step will increase your confidence. If not, read on.

Limber up. Even a well-prepared student will need to warm up for the examination by conducting a review. Review course work by setting up a reasonable work schedule and then following it (with some flexibility, of course).

Review does not mean reread. Review should be refreshing, just as a warm-up exercise is meant to get you ready for more and not to drain you of energy. Review is just part of the routine. Look through your notes and your texts, as well as your past essays and tests. This process will be easier if you have highlighted important points beforehand (and if you have done all the required work in the first place).

Locate problem areas. To overcome shyness about the exam, you must confront your fears. Ask yourself, unflinchingly, what are you afraid of? If you find that you are worried about some specific problems in your understanding of the course, pay particular attention to these. The benefits will be twofold: you will conquer some of your fear, and you will learn something.

Making the material fit

In order to learn anything, you must make it a part of yourself. You must carry it away with you and get carried away with it (while still keeping your feet on the ground).

To gain full possession of the course material, you will use **memory, fluency, application,** and **imagination.** Here's how.

Memory. There is no learning without memory, though memory is just the first step in turning course material into something of your own. To sharpen your skills of recall, try reading aloud, so that both sight and hearing can register the information.

Concentrate on facts and significant details. Help your memory along by making associations or by visualizing material. These tactics will trigger memory when you're stuck for words.

If memorizing is not your strong point, don't despair. Although an essay exam demands that you have some facts at your fingertips, how the facts are presented, how they are used, and what you create out of them are equally important.

Fluency. To make yourself an expert in a discipline, learn how to speak its language as you master its content. Make the terms a part of your language, by learning to define them, by including them in speech, and by using them in writing. When imagining how you would answer a question, talk to yourself. Jot down notes. The more conversant you are with specialized language in your subject area, the more gracefully you will write under pressure.

Application. Make sure you can use what you know. To apply your knowledge, you need to supply a context. Don't just repeat the facts: question the material. As you review, note questions that the textbook may have raised. Keep in mind any questions raised in class or topics distributed for review that strike you as pertinent. These may prove useful when exam time comes.

Imagination. All work and no play would make a dull examination and certainly a grim study period. Approach the test and your preparation for it with a sense of play, if it all possible. Wonder about its potential. Don't confine your imagination to the tried and true; experiment with some ideas of your own. Develop a theory or two, as if you were preparing for a formal essay. You may well get a chance to try them out on the examination. The difference between an A and a B is often a desire to develop your own ideas and to create something new out of the material.

Taking the plunge

Writing an examination successfully depends on two factors: what you know *and* what you can say about it in a limited time. To make the best use of your time, follow this basic pattern: **read, sketch, write, skim.**

Read the questions carefully. Before you get your feet wet, so to speak, read over the entire exam. Take careful note of the instructions. If you are given a choice of questions, devote a few minutes to their selection. Allot an appropriate amount of time for each question and *adhere to that schedule*. It is wise to begin with the questions you know best.

Look for questions to challenge you. Remember that an essay question does not necessarily have a correct answer. An essay simply tries, as its name suggests, to come to terms with a provocative, perhaps troubling, question.

Become familiar with these common examination terms:

Explain

If you are asked to *explain*, be thorough in your approach and ready to clarify in detail, as though you were teaching the reader. Both structure and substance are needed, so be prepared to show both breadth and depth in your treatment of the question.

Example

> The federal Progressive Conservative Party has been called the "normal opposition party." Explain. What must the federal Progressive Conservative Party do to become the "normal government party"?

Begin by using facts to explain the label of "normal opposition party." These facts should be available to you from the course material. Then, making sure to refer to appropriate sources, discuss various theories of what is needed to ensure Conservative success at the polls.

Discuss

If asked to *discuss*, use the latitude of the question to focus on some part of the problem that captures your attention and allows you to present a lively, informative, and thoughtful consideration of the problem. Treat the question as if you were writing a less than formal essay—as indeed you are.

Example

> Discuss the ways in which family ties and loyalties dramatically expand the inner conflicts and crises of conscience in Huckleberry Finn and King Lear.

Begin by focussing on the conventional bond between parents and children. Show how the bonds are broken in both works. Then you could go on to show how a new sense of family is created for both Lear and Huck in the levelling process that occurs in both works. Remember to include many examples to support your points.

Outline

If asked to *outline*, put your emphasis on the bare bones of the argument—the facts—rather than the flesh. An outline will require you to place more stress on the shape and the sequence of your subject, rather than the substance.

Example

Outline how and why geographical factors are so strongly evident in classical mythology.

Your outline should be broadly based, isolating a number of examples of geographical factors in a variety of myths, rather than in one or two. Follow these examples with a discussion suggesting some of the reasons for this phenomenon. Aim at broad coverage rather than deep analysis.

Compare and Contrast

If asked to *compare and contrast*, or simply to *compare*, remember that the object is to show the relationship between two things. Focus the essay on the connections and differences you find by setting two things side by side in your sketch.

Example

Compare and contrast the women's movement of the late nineteenth and early twentieth centuries with the women's movement which began in the late 1960s.

Begin by making an outline to discover the main similarities and differences. Say, for example, that the main similarities include the desire to change attitudes toward working women and the desire to gain more influence in the workplace. The differences might include the earlier movement's focus on political rights and the later movement's focus on issues relating to sexual harassment on the job. You could compare and contrast not only the goals of the movements, but also the relative success of each of them. Then you need a summary of your findings, in order to compare these two movements more generally.

Sketch

Sketch out your answers to the questions chosen. First, let yourself go. Jot things down helter-skelter as they occur to you. Then, try to gather material into categories for discussion. Avoid getting embroiled in outlines too complex or too demanding for the time allowed.

Sketch your answers in the briefest possible form. As you do so, use key words in the question to guide your responses. Above all, obey the terms of the question as you work in the things you want to say.

Write

Sketching your material enabled you to get warmed up. Therefore, the writing process itself should be more graceful and more organized. To ensure an organized presentation, fall back on established essay-writing habits. Begin at the beginning. Make sure your answer has an introduction, a body, and a conclusion. While these sections will be hastier and less polished, do not abandon structure entirely.

The main thing to keep in mind is the connections you are making between the question and the knowledge you brought with you into the exam.

Refer to your sketch and to the original question as you write, but also allow yourself the freedom of an unexpected idea or a unique turn of phrase, as long as it doesn't interfere with the basic flow of your answer.

Let the words flow, but keep the writing legible. Write on every other line as a courtesy to your reader.

Skim

Force yourself to read your answers quickly and to make small changes. To neglect this stage is to force your instructor to become the proofreader—a proofreader who might become annoyed at your carelessness. A small mistake is forgivable; reckless abandon is not.

Standing out in a crowd

Now that you know how to pass an essay examination, you may well wonder how to surpass expectations. Though you are writing the examination along with perhaps hundreds of other students, there are ways of making your exam style unique without defying the conventions of test writing.

What does a bleary-eyed instructor, marking two hundred essay questions, look for in an answer?

Definition. An essay examination is your chance to show your understanding of how some terminology in the subject area works. Unlike a multiple-choice exam, this kind of test will allow you to use the language of the discipline precisely and fluently.

Direction. Your answers should be pointed directly at the questions. Don't make the mistake of trying to say everything; you can't assume that the instructor will give you credit if he or she can find the right answer somewhere in your paper. You also can't assume that your instructor will want to look for your answer. Make your answer easy to find.

Detail. While even an exceptional student cannot remember all of the fine points in a complex body of work, it is certainly possible to learn a smattering of appropriate details on a variety of subjects. Such details may be inserted, where applicable, as you are writing the exam. Details have the effect of a close-up. They allow you to focus on something precise, and they reveal your careful reading of your subject matter.

Depth. To demonstrate depth of knowledge, an examination must show that the writer has thought about the implications of the subject and of the specific question. Dive in. Don't avoid entirely the deeper complexities of a question in favour of its superficial requirements. Where possible, do more than you need to do. Answer questions seriously; you are writing as a curious and concerned expert. Address your subject, not as an illustration of how well you have learned it, but rather as a serious attempt to advance the subject matter itself.

Discovery. A brilliant exam will show what a student has learned above and beyond what the instructor has taught. If you have some insight or even some questions about the material that have not been raised in class, this is your opportunity to voice them. Never recite the answer to a question based on your memory of a lecture unless you have, sadly, nothing of your own to add to the material. An exam should occasionally allow you to take intelligent, calculated risks.

■ The Informal Essay—Essay as Colleague

> Every vital development in language is a development of feeling as well.
>
> *T.S. Eliot*

In most cases, the essays you write as part of your course work will be formal in tone. When you are allowed the luxury of writing an informal essay, follow these basic suggestions:

1. Be yourself
2. Choose a comfortable subject
3. Experiment with style and subject
4. Shop around

■ The Role of the Informal Essay

The informal essay affords you greater freedom and a more casual approach than the formal essay. Although the same writing process is demanded in the informal essay—it too needs a thesis statement, a typical essay shape, and a command of the mechanics of writing—what you say and how you say it are a matter of invention rather than convention.

AUDIENCE: friendly company who find your perspective stimulating

PURPOSE: to talk about anything that appeals to your imagination

Be yourself

The informal essay should let the reader learn about you and about your subject. Whereas you are obliged to keep a restrained and professional distance in the formal essay, you should maintain a casual and personal tone in the informal essay. Someone reading your paper will learn not only the facts and figures of your subject, but also some of your characteristics and your attitudes.

You will necessarily be more exposed: flaws in your arguments, biases in your attitudes, and unattractive aspects of your personality may show. The informal essay is by definition a face-to-face meeting between you and the reader. To prevent excessive vulnerability, you must examine your attitudes scrupulously, and be prepared to face your reader's reaction—alone.

Choose a comfortable subject

Whereas a formal essay must be logical, objective, tight, and well supported, an informal essay allows you to be more subjective in your viewpoint, more personal in your selection of supporting material, and more idio-syncratic in your approach.

The formal essay may argue a life-and-death matter; the informal essay is, by contrast, an intellectual exercise for its own sake. This characterization does not mean that the informal essay cannot be heartfelt or deeply impor-tant—but its tone is less public, its argument closer to your personal interests, and its value less dependent on knowledge of facts than on grace and eloquence.

Experiment with subject and style

You must draw the material and the viewpoint from your own sense of the subject, rather than looking to authorities for defence.

In an informal essay, your object is to keep your reader interested in what you have to say. You cannot assume that the subject is intrinsically appealing to the reader from a professional standpoint, as you do in the formal essay. Since the material you choose in the informal essay reflects you and your personal understanding of the matter, you must appeal to your reader person-ally and share your opinions enthusiastically.

The informal essay allows you the opportunity to experiment with lan-guage in a way that would not be appropriate in a formal or research essay. Try writing as you speak—without lapsing into grammatical and structural errors. For example, in an informal essay, you can use contractions (don't, can't, etc.), which are generally not acceptable in a formal essay.

Shop around

Make an effort to read some personal essays, whether newspaper editorials or in magazines or the "collected works" of a classmate. Here are some choices for stylistic study:

Woody Allen	Allan Fotheringham
Harry Bruce	Joey Slinger
Michele Landsberg	Lewis Thomas
Russell Baker	Ray Guy
Fran Lebowitz	James Thurber

The Literary Essay—Essay as Analyst

> Looking back, I imagine I was always writing.
> Twaddle it was too. But better far write twaddle
> or anything, anything, than nothing at all.
> *Katherine Mansfield*

The literary essay requires you to read, to analyze, and to come to terms with the meaning of a piece of literature. Whether it demands secondary sources or simply focusses on the literary work itself, the literary essay demands that you show your understanding of how and why the work is put together the way it is.

Write the literary essay according to the following stages:

1. Formulate a thesis about the work
2. Read the work closely
3. Use secondary sources, if required
4. Select only the best supporting evidence
5. Quote often, but not at great length
6. Write in the present tense
7. Write with both the text and the argument in mind
8. Revise with style

AUDIENCE: someone who has read the novel, or poem, or short story, but who wants to understand more about how it works (for example, its structure, its themes, its techniques)

PURPOSE: to interpret the meaning of a work and the techniques by which that meaning is revealed

Formulate a thesis

The thesis of the literary essay should be something that helps the reader make sense of the work in question.

For example, in Joseph Conrad's *Heart of Darkness*, the reader needs to know why Conrad includes the passage in which Knights, the first narrator, and Marlow, the second narrator, discuss the Thames river. Your viewpoint on this question will determine your interpretation of the work's meaning.

Find your thesis by asking yourself what the important questions are about the literary work you have in front of you. Sometimes these will be assigned, but sometimes you will have to find your own questions, based on class discussion and reading.

Remember that you cannot conclusively prove your thesis statement. All you are expected to do is to show that your reasons for it are based on the text itself.

Read the work closely

With your working thesis in mind, read the work carefully. Underlining or highlighting the text as you go along is often a good idea (provided you own it, of course).

Note anything that might count as evidence for your analysis of the characteristics of a literary work. Don't, however, neglect passages that might support a contrary view. You will need to account for these as well.

Use secondary sources, if required

Maintain your balance when using secondary sources. Use them to get some critical perspective on the work in question, but remember that your own task is no different from theirs. The main reason for writing a literary essay is to show your own powers of analysis.

Keep track of the sources you have consulted. The ideas you find must be acknowledged to avoid charges of plagiarism. Keep track also of the basic line of argument set forth by each critic you consult: it is unfair to take ideas or phrasing if you intend to use them out of their original context.

Select only the best evidence

After close reading, you need to "back off" from the work somewhat. Your task is not to summarize the work, or to explain every detail of it, but merely to present a viewpoint that suggests what the work means and how it is put together.

Skim through the work, noting down the most prominent support you have found. Then, categorize the material into sections appropriate for discussion in your essay. Fit these into a rough outline, and you are ready to write.

Example

> Thesis statement: Conrad includes the discussion of the Thames so that the reader will become aware of the effects of conquest on the conquered as well as the conquerors.
> A. Knights sees the Thames as symbolic of the light of civilization; Marlow sees it as symbolic of savagery.
> B. Knights is romantic and patriotic about England's empire; Marlow calls to mind ancient times when England was conquered by the Roman Empire.
> C. Knights, like the readers, modifies his view of the Thames in response to Marlow's narrative.

To stress that the two narratives are meant to parallel the reader's change in perspective as they read, the last point focusses on the alteration in Knights's view of the river near the end of the work.

As you gather support, try not to include everything. Pick only those passages central to an understanding of the work's meaning and those that work best as illustrations of your thesis.

Quote often, but not at great length

The best illustration of a point in a literary essay is a quotation. Whereas paraphrase may be a useful way of reporting research, the quotation is the most precise way to examine meaning in literature. Exactitude is important.

Remember, though, that you must *use* your quotations. Don't just copy them and assume that your point has been made. Focus in on them to show exactly how they work as support for your thesis. Don't assume that the meaning of the quotations or your purpose in quoting them is self-evident.

Write in the present tense

When discussing a work of literature, stay in the present tense—treat the work as a living thing.

Example

> Knights describes the river in romantic terms.

Write with both text and argument in mind

Stay close to the text at all times. But remember that you are not writing to record the plot or to state the obvious. Assume that the reader has read the work. Your job is to offer an interpretation of its meaning. Use the primary text to *demonstrate* your thesis and present your support for the argument at every step of the way.

Write an analysis, not an appreciation or a summary. Don't, for example, waste words admiring Conrad's skill as a novelist. Instead, show how a particular literary work is put together and explain why it has the effect it does.

Assume that the work has unity and coherence, unless evidence shows otherwise. Take the text apart and show how some features of it work. Your job is to show how its synthesis is achieved.

Revise with style

In a literary essay, style is crucial. Your grade will depend not only on what you say but also on how you say it. Check for grace in style. Aim at writing smoothly and confidently. Find a critic you admire and emulate his or her method of proceeding. Your argument, no matter how cogent, will not succeed unless your paper is written well.

The following is a sample literary essay whose format conforms to the new MLA guidelines. Refer to the section Documenting — MLA, APA, and University of Chicago Guidelines, pp. 136-47 for more information. Study it carefully, noting the format and the method of documentation.

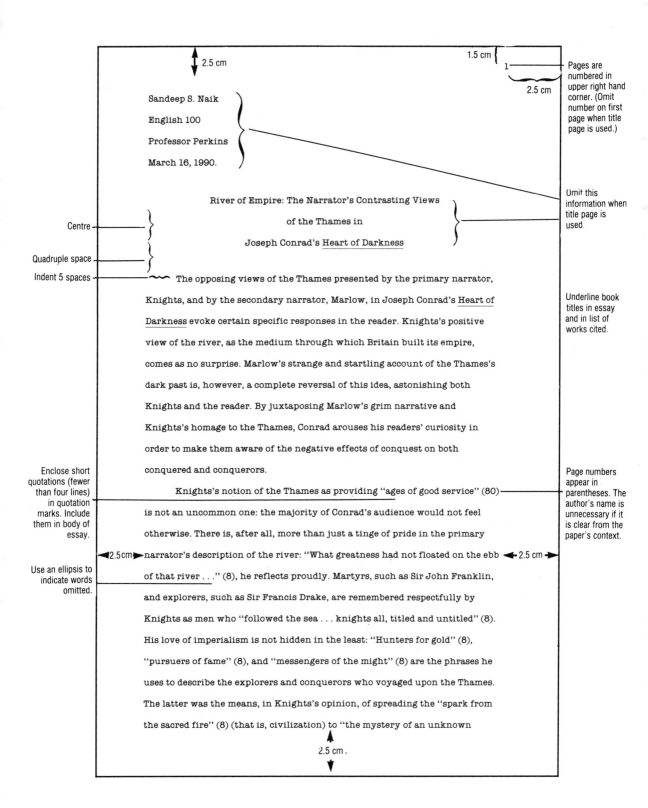

2.5 cm

1.5 cm

1

2.5 cm

Pages are numbered in upper right hand corner. (Omit number on first page when title page is used.)

Sandeep S. Naik

English 100

Professor Perkins

March 16, 1990.

Omit this information when title page is used.

River of Empire: The Narrator's Contrasting Views

of the Thames in

Joseph Conrad's <u>Heart of Darkness</u>

Centre

Quadruple space

Indent 5 spaces

The opposing views of the Thames presented by the primary narrator, Knights, and by the secondary narrator, Marlow, in Joseph Conrad's <u>Heart of Darkness</u> evoke certain specific responses in the reader. Knights's positive view of the river, as the medium through which Britain built its empire, comes as no surprise. Marlow's strange and startling account of the Thames's dark past is, however, a complete reversal of this idea, astonishing both Knights and the reader. By juxtaposing Marlow's grim narrative and Knights's homage to the Thames, Conrad arouses his readers' curiosity in order to make them aware of the negative effects of conquest on both conquered and conquerors.

Underline book titles in essay and in list of works cited.

Knights's notion of the Thames as providing "ages of good service" (80) is not an uncommon one: the majority of Conrad's audience would not feel otherwise. There is, after all, more than just a tinge of pride in the primary

2.5cm narrator's description of the river: "What greatness had not floated on the ebb 2.5 cm

of that river . . ." (8), he reflects proudly. Martyrs, such as Sir John Franklin, and explorers, such as Sir Francis Drake, are remembered respectfully by Knights as men who "followed the sea . . . knights all, titled and untitled" (8). His love of imperialism is not hidden in the least: "Hunters for gold" (8), "pursuers of fame" (8), and "messengers of the might" (8) are the phrases he uses to describe the explorers and conquerors who voyaged upon the Thames. The latter was the means, in Knights's opinion, of spreading the "spark from the sacred fire" (8) (that is, civilization) to "the mystery of an unknown

Enclose short quotations (fewer than four lines) in quotation marks. Include them in body of essay.

Use an ellipsis to indicate words omitted.

Page numbers appear in parentheses. The author's name is unnecessary if it is clear from the paper's context.

2.5 cm .

earth'' (8), such as Africa. Indeed, without the Thames, the ''seed of commonwealths, the germ of empires'' (8) could never have been planted.

Marlow's strange and startling account of the Thames's dark past is quite different. The ''sacred fire'' (8) Knights values so deeply is just ''a flash of lightning in the clouds . . . [a] flicker'' (9) in Marlow's eyes. To him it is darkness that has prevailed, a darkness symbolized by the Thames. He substantiates this view by presenting the other side of imperialism; the darkness and misery associated with, and inflicted on, the vanquished. It was the Thames that brought the Romans, says Marlow, to a land of ''cold, fog, tempests, disease and death'' (10), a far cry from the empire it would one day become. There are no Sir John Franklins or Sir Francis Drakes in Marlow's view, only ''the utter savagery . . . of wild men'' (10). Whereas Knights associates the Thames with calmness, serenity, and tranquillity, Marlow believes it led to danger, evil, death, and destruction: ''No Falernian wine here'' (10), Marlow says, rejecting the glory and heroism that Knights embraces. For Marlow, there is only ''death skulking in the air . . . [men] dying like flies . . . the incomprehensible'' (10).

Though vastly different, the opinions of Marlow and Knights are not unrelated by any means. Knights presents imperialism from a romantic perspective, full of the praise and respect he has for his native land. For him, it is the heart of an empire. By presenting this aspect first, Conrad subtly allows the readers to participate in this familiar view. Almost immediately after, though, the readers face Marlow's idea of the Thames as the means by which the Romans were able to capture the ''unknown earth'' (8) that would one day be Britain. Marlow describes a Thames of ''nineteen hundred years ago'' (9) when Britain was not the conqueror but the conquered, a complete turnabout of the patriotic perspective, and one unfamiliar to most readers. Conrad exploits this unfamiliarity to change the readers' point of view.

Such a response from the readers is critical to the rest of the novel. From this point on, the readers have questions about the experiences that have led Marlow to see the Thames in this light. This first difference of

Use square brackets to add words needed for clarity.

opinion leads to Marlow's account of his life in Africa amidst "all that mysterious life of the wilderness that stirs in the forest" (10). Marlow's view of the Thames's history also sets the tone for the story that follows: it introduces the contrast between growth and destruction, the conquerors and the conquered, the civilized and the savage, and of light versus darkness.

The readers, like Knights, are affected by Marlow's view of the Thames and by the narrative that follows. In the end, Knights sees the Thames in a changed light: though still "leading to the uttermost ends of the earth" (76), the river now "flowed sombre under an overcast sky–[where it] seemed to lead into the heart of an immense darkness" (76). By using the double narration, Conrad has created a character in Knights whose response to Marlow's account of the Thames, and to his story, serves as a guide to our own. In this manner, Conrad manipulates us in the hope that Knights's new-found awareness of the price of imperialism is also our own.

List according to
last name and in
alphabetical
order.

List only works
cited in essay.

Abbreviate
publication
information
without
sacrificing clarity.

Works Cited

Conrad, Joseph. Heart of Darkness. Ed. Robert Kimbrough. 3rd ed. New York:

Norton, 1988.

■ The Book Review—Essay as Critic

> Writing . . . keeps me from believing every-
> thing I read.
>
> *Gloria Steinem*

Most of the book reviews you will be asked to write have a more specific purpose than the kind you see in newspapers and magazines. You will be asked not only to report on the content of a book and to evaluate it, but also to analyze it in terms of its contribution to the discipline. A book review gives you a chance to examine one potential source in a given area, often as a prelude to writing a research essay. Like any other essay, it demands a thesis statement that clarifies your reaction to the book.

If you are asked to review a book as part of a course requirement, select a book with a subject matter that appeals to you and with which you feel comfortable. Proceed according to the following stages:

1. Describe or summarize the contents of the book
2. Describe and evaluate its tactics
3. Consider its contribution
4. Illustrate your argument
5. Maintain your critical balance

To write a focussed book review, remember your role as fair-minded and helpful critic.

■ The Role of the Book Review

Like other essays, the book review's form is determined by its readers and its function.

AUDIENCE: someone who has not read the book, but who is interested in its subject matter and has some background in the discipline

PURPOSE: to summarize, analyze, and evaluate a book, and to show your critical acumen in so doing; then, to recommend, to criticize, or to dismiss the book according to careful judgment

Describe the Book

1. Determine the thesis of the book (if it is a critical text), the theme (or general meaning) of the book (if it is not), and the audience for which the book is intended.
2. Summarize the book's contents briefly, without giving the show away.
3. Use the book's preface, introduction, and table of contents as a rough guide for your discussion of the work.
4. Discuss the general purpose of the book, without getting caught up in too much detail.

Neil Postman, in his book Teaching as a Conserving Activity *(1979), argues that the function of formal education should be to counteract the biases of the culture, rather than to reinforce them. To illustrate this point, he focusses on the pervasive influence of television and other media and recommends that education teach society to be more critical of the media. Postman intends this book to be a modification of his earlier work,* Teaching as a Subversive Activity *(1969), in which he advocated innovation. In this book, his argument is that education must work against the unthinking forces of change that prevail in the culture as a whole.*

Describe and evaluate the book's tactics

1. If the book is a critical text, describe its method of argument. If it is not a critical text, describe the techniques by which the material is presented.
2. Note how well the book does what it sets out to do.
3. Note what else might have been done or what might have been done differently.
4. Note why you liked (or disliked) the book.

Example

The book sets out to show how television has affected our way of seeing the world. It argues that television has made us less conscious of the past, that it has lowered our attention span, and that it has made us more susceptible to "quick-fix" solutions to problems—as a consequence of too much exposure to television commercials, which reduce life to shallow and easily remedied problems.

Postman insists that the way to counter this problem is to teach people about the media and about how the media alter our perceptions of things. He argues that the development of strong critical-thinking skills will put a stop to the passivity and superficiality of the cultural attitudes provoked by television viewing.

The chief flaw in Postman's approach is his own lack of sources. Given that he advocates critical appraisal of the means by which information is conveyed, the onus is on him to show that some of the effects of television that he lists are, in fact, present.

Consider the book's contribution

1. Compare the book to others you have read with a similar thesis or theme.
2. Ask yourself what you learned from the book.

Example

Teaching as a Conserving Activity *seems to present a useful corrective to the problems of value in education today. Postman points to some real dangers created by the commercialization of the media and emphasizes the role that education must play in maintaining old values in society as well as espousing new ones.*

Illustrate your argument

1. At every step of the way, use snippets from the book to back up your position and to give the reader a taste of the work.
2. Include both positive and negative illustrations, unless, of course, your review is entirely positive or negative (rarely the case).
3. Be sure to integrate your illustrations from the book as part of your argument, and not simply as decoration.

Example

Although some of the charges Postman makes about the negative effects of television are justified— such as its invasion of privacy and its stress on seeing things from the outside, superficially rather than analytically— some of his charges are exaggerated. When he claims that television is not analytic because it is "picture-centered,"[1] he argues that we cannot prove a picture true or false the way we can a proposition. But Postman here is comparing apples and oranges. Words are not always used to create propositions either; sometimes they tell stories, just as pictures do, and these stories cannot be categorized as being true or false either. The fault, if there is one, does not lie with the medium, but instead, perhaps, with the use to which it is put. In other words, television in itself does not automatically lead to a deterioration in critical-thinking skills.

Maintain your critical balance

1. Don't be intimidated by ideas just because they are in print. Your object is to assess the merits of the book in question.
2. Don't be too harsh in your judgments. Remember that the author deserves mercy as well as justice.

Example

Ultimately, Postman's position that education should move to counteract some of the biases of the culture is a valid one: some of his arguments for it, however, need more support and closer critical scrutiny than he has given them.

■ The Research Essay—Essay as Explorer

> Language is the archives of history.
> *Ralph Waldo Emerson*

A research paper is a formal essay based on your exploration of other people's ideas, rather than simply an analysis of your own thoughts. Although both the expository essay and the persuasive essay may use source material to some extent, the research essay is unique. Its purpose is to formulate a thesis based on a survey and assessment of source material.

The following steps are essential to the development of a research paper:

1. Mapping out the area of exploration
2. Finding a working bibliography
3. Drawing up an outline
4. Recording source material
5. Writing and documenting your essay

■ The Role of the Research Paper

A research paper must be modified to suit its readers and its special aims.

AUDIENCE: an informed, curious reader, whom you address on a professional level

PURPOSE:　to demonstrate your skill in exploring, evaluating, and recording source material in a manner that shows how you have synthesized it

Mapping out the area of exploration

Before you begin to explore the library, you must find a subject area that is appropriate for investigation. A good research topic will have the following characteristics:

1. **Scope.** Your subject should be neither too broad nor too narrow in its focus.

Example

---

the use of home videos—too broad
a comparison of home videos and films—not focussed enough
the adaptation of Hollywood films to suit the new specifications of the video format—more focussed

2. **Support.** Your subject must be treated in written (and, in this case, film) sources that are available to you. For example, a recent subject may not be a good choice because there may not yet be enough written about it. Also, remember that your sources must be treated objectively, so that the final paper reflects what is known about a subject, rather than just what you believe to be true about a subject. For example, your discussion of innovations in the film industry must deal with the techniques of filmmaking rather than just with their impact.

3. **Significance.** Find something that you want to explore and that needs exploration. It would not, for instance, be enough to announce that you were going to list the new techniques by which filmmakers adapt their works to the small screen. You would need to explain how these techniques achieve the desired effects.

Finding a working bibliography

Read widely at first to locate the best sources. Then read deeply in order to get at the heart of the matter. Explore the topic with your tentative thesis in mind, revising it as you go along.

1. Find general information in an encyclopedia, dictionary, or other reference book. The list in the Appendix offers some places to start. Remember, though, that these general sources only scratch the surface.

2. Find information in the library computer system, microfiche, or card catalogue. Look under the subject heading or use the names of authors or titles that you have found in any of the encyclopedias you consulted.

   In the case at hand, to find information on filmmaking, look up FILM or VIDEO under the subject heading in the library card catalogue or on the computer.

3. Consult periodical indexes for further information. Often the

periodical will give you more current material than is available in books. Some indexes are listed in the Appendix.

4. As an alternative to looking through indexes and abstracts for information on a subject, you can have a search performed for you by computer. Most college and university libraries have an on-line search service.

   The advantages of a computer search are that it is quick, thorough, and up-to-date. In most college and university libraries, there is a charge for having this service performed. There are many factors that affect the cost of a search, such as the complexity of the search strategy, the cost of the database(s) searched, the number of references found and printed, and even the time of day. Nevertheless, most searches required by an undergraduate student should cost only $5 to $15. Your library's on-line searcher can usually give you an estimate before beginning the search.

   The whole field of using computers to find information is changing very rapidly. The best way to know what is happening RIGHT NOW is to ask your reference librarian, who will bring you up-to-date on the technology and, more importantly, the choices available in your particular college or university library.

5. Examine your sources with your specific topic in mind. Check the table of contents and the index of the books you find to search for suitable material.

6. Note down bibliographical information for any of the sources you consult. Small note cards (3" x 5") are useful. Record the library call numbers for your sources.

7. Follow the rules of documentation that apply to your discipline at this stage, and you will save time and trouble toward the end. Some guides to acceptable documentation are listed in the Appendix.

SAMPLE BIBLIOGRAPHY CARD

> Gibaldi, Joseph, and Walter S. Achtert.
> <u>MLA Handbook for Writers of Research Papers</u>. 3rd. ed. New York: Modern Language Association, 1984.

Although the sample research essay shown in this book is in the style of the American Psychological Association, some disciplines demand other styles of documentation. For example, English instructors often require that an essay's format follow the guidelines of the Modern Language Association, as shown in the sample literary essay on p. 73. Ask your instructor if in doubt.

Drawing up an outline

An outline for a research essay takes its direction from your preparatory reading. Follow the instructions in Chapter 3 on how to design an outline with these precautions in mind:

1. Your outline must be flexible enough to accommodate all the information pertinent to your thesis statement.
2. Your outline must be fair and must reflect an objective approach to the material.
3. Your outline must be firmly established in your mind so that it does not attempt to include more material than can be adequately handled within the limits of the assignment.
4. Your outline is designed to be used. In the case of a research essay, the outline dictates the direction of your note-taking. It should help you stay on track in your explorations and help you limit yourself to what is possible.

Recording source material

Like an explorer, you must accurately record the steps of your journey. You need a system. Here are some suggestions to simplify the task:

1. Take notes on large index cards (4" x 6" should do).
2. Identify the source on each card as briefly as possible. Usually, a last name and a page number will do.
3. Quote or paraphrase as the occasion demands (remember that too much quotation is dull). In addition, paraphrasing as you read will help you make sense of the material.
4. Limit yourself generally to one note per card to make sorting easier. This tactic will keep you from unconsciously relying too heavily on any one source.
5. Sort through your material at intervals to decide where it will fit into your working outline. If it won't fit, revise the outline or throw the irrelevant information out—no matter how attractive it is.
6. Copy accurately. If the passage is very lengthy, photocopy it to ensure precision, but be aware of copyright laws.

Why bother?

Note-taking is such a painful chore that it is tempting not to do it. Don't succumb to the temptation. Note-taking is an essential part of research. It will help you determine the value of your sources. Ask these questions as you take notes:

1. Are the sources reliable?
2. Are they recent?
3. Are the sources themselves respected and well reviewed by others?
4. What are your own reactions to the sources?

This last point shows the need to record your own reactions to source material as your proceed. Add these ideas to your note cards to help you develop ideas later. You can differentiate them from source material by adding your initials.

Remember, the object of research is not to record facts, but to evaluate and synthesize your findings about an unsettled matter according to the viewpoint or thesis of your paper.

Writing and documenting your essay

Prepare an outline, complete with intended patterns of argument, as suggested in Chapters 3 and 4 of this text. Then, write the first draft of your essay's introduction, body, and conclusion. This time, however, you must make sure to acknowledge your debt to any source as you write. One good way to do so is to include an abbreviated version of the source in parentheses immediately following the quoted matter in your essay.

Example

The letterbox image can appear truly diminutive on any but the largest video screens, and the large blank spaces above and below the image can be very distracting. Further, by using little more than half the available screen space, image resolution in letterbox format is almost cut in half (Strain, p. 564).

This example not only shows the ease of abbreviation, but also demonstrates the ease of the APA style of documentation. It is also an example of the benefits of good preliminary note-taking.

For more information on documentation in MLA, APA, and traditional footnote style, see Chapter 16.

Control

The special challenge of the research paper is to handle your source material in a controlled way. To control your research essay, remember these guidelines:

1. **Keep it limited.** Qualify the aim of your essay and stay within the limits of the thesis and the assignment.

2. **Keep it concise.** Avoid pretentious diction.
   (See Chapter 15 for more information.)

3. **Keep it formal.** This suggestion may even mean that you should not use the pronoun "I," in order to maintain objectivity (although it is often acceptable to do so). Ask your instructor for specific advice on this point.

4. **Keep it clean.** Small errors reduce the essay's credibility as an accurate record of research.

5. **Make it yours.** Don't lose yourself in assembled bits of research. Assimilate the material. Learn from it. What you include and how you use it determine your success as a researcher.

■ Sample Research Essay

The following is a sample research essay whose format conforms to the new APA guidelines. Study it carefully, noting the format and the method of documentation.

Freeze Frame:

A Study of the Impact of Video on Hollywood Movie Production

Marty Chan

Film 210

Jean Underwood

April 4, 1990

Whether or not Hollywood filmmakers appreciate the home video market, they have acknowledged its existence by the way they produce their movies. They have initiated changes in the technology, composition, and directing of their films to accommodate the films' release on video. By implementing these changes, they hope to retain the aesthetic quality of their films in the transfer from the large movie screen to the smaller television screen.

One of the primary concerns in the film-to-video transfer is reduced picture quality; film images lose their subtleties of colour and "coalesce into monochromatic blocks" (Chute, 1984, p. 49) when reproduced as video images. A film, like a painting, is complete with textures and shades that present a natural image; however, video is a photograph that captures only vivid colours, thus creating an artificial picture. This reduction in contrast diminishes the film's effectiveness on tape, particularly in low-lighting sequences, which Shane (1953) demonstrates: elements of composition disappear in the film's countless low-lit scenes; additionally, the dusk, dawn, and night scenes look almost identical – all dim – thus creating problems in establishing the time frame.

Technology sheds light on this problem. Today's filmstock speed has been raised from ASA 100 to as high as ASA 800, a change which increases the film's light sensitivity, enabling it to record more shades. Multilayer emulsions and flattened-molecule technology reduce the graininess that is visible with higher-speed filmstock; furthermore, improved lenses compensate for the faster film's lower resolving power – the ability to record fine detail. These innovations enrich the picture quality of film and video images.

In the actual process of transferring the film to video, other developments have been incorporated. The arrival of the colour telecine in 1977 made the video translation of colour films possible, and subsequent

Use the abbreviation p. for "page", pp. for "pages".

improvements to the equipment, which reduced the tearing and scratching of the original prints, improved the visual quality of the transferred images. Another development has been low-contrast, or telecine-optimized, print film. Specifically designed for use with telecines, this film is cheaper and translates low-lit images faithfully. ABC Films used the low-contrast print film for Silkwood to cut down production costs:

> For example, when ABC Films produced Silkwood, the lab was able to make both theatrical and low-contrast prints at the same time, with no cost premium. The low-contrast prints were used for mastering video cassettes for the home VCR market. (Schafer, 1986, p. 99)

First reference normally includes the author's name, date of publication, and page number.

An alternative to low-contrast film is interpositive prints – positive images copied from the negative – that allow the filmmaker to protect his original negatives and still retain picture quality:

> When striving to preserve in the video transfer all the fine nuances of highlights and shadow, one discovers that some scenes look better when transferred from an interpositive print rather than from a low-cost answer print. Particularly very dark night scenes may benefit from this treatment. (Malkiewicz, 1989, p. 192)

Indent quotations of four lines or more.

Though these innovations have improved the picture quality of videos, few solutions exist to facilitate the squeezing of a wide-screen movie into the small box of a television. One solution is cropping – the trimming of the film frame at the sides, the top, and bottom so that it fits on a video frame. Often, this process includes chopping off characters from the waist down and trimming off the tops of their heads, replacing the original wide-screen panoramic shot with a cramped, claustrophobic image. The video image travels back and forth across the film frame to follow the vital action, which results in a "pan and scan' television print" (Strain, p. 560).

However, filmmakers react negatively to the cropping of their work for video release. They believe that the process lessens the effectiveness of film language; it alters original cinematography and editing; and it unnecessarily imposes the will of the camera upon the viewer. An illustration of this point can be seen in the translation of a stable shot of three people into a video image (Strain). Because the smaller frame can contain only two people simultaneously, it must pan from person to person over the course of the trio's interaction, disrupting the original stable shot and eliminating visual elements from the frame's edges. Before the video transfer, the viewer could shift her focus among the three characters and note their facial expressions at whim; now, the camera manipulates her vision and emphasizes reactions that may not have been intended in the original shot.

The mural screen format, or letterboxing, circumvents these problems; it presents the entire wide-screen image on the video frame, but on a much smaller scale. So small is the scale that it is about half the height of a normal video image. Blank spaces occupy the areas above and below the image, creating the sense that one is watching a movie from the opposite end zone of a football field. The earliest evidence of this format is a Disneyland television show promoting Sleeping Beauty (Strain, p. 564); more recently, Innerspace was presented in this format. The advantage of this format is that it retains the original cinematography and editing; the disadvantage is its small size:

> The letterbox image can appear truly diminutive on any but the largest video screens, and the large blank spaces above and below the image can be very distracting. Further, by using little more than half the available screen space, image resolution in letterbox format is almost cut in half. (Strain, p. 564)

Neither cropping nor letterboxing appeals to filmmakers as a concrete solution for preserving cinematography in the film-to-video transfer. Ultimately, the solution rests in their hands. They must decide whether they are shooting film for release in the theatre or on video. If they consider video as a viable market, they must keep compositional elements away from the edges of the film frame; the "mise-en-scene" (the way the picture is composed) must become more central. According to Charges Eidsvik (1988), "All films must be composed for what the Europeans call 'amphibious' life, for viewability both on theatre and on television screens" (p. 21).

Most mainstream Hollywood movies released today are adapted for video release; in these cases, the filmmakers sacrifice "mise-en-scene" on the large screen so that the video release has better composition. Karate Kid, Part II (1986), Three Men and a Baby (1987), and Big (1988) represent a few of the commercial movies that succeeded both in the theatres and on video; however, their cinematography suggests they were intended primarily for video release: tight medium shots from the waist up, close-ups, and central "mise-en-scene" dominate these films.

Another change in composition for the sake of video is the reduction of long static shots and the increase of moving shots. The purpose for this is, as Eidsvik claims, that "TV screens do not carry enough visual information for long-held static shots to retain viewer attention" (p. 21). Also, film has a selective depth of field, while video has an infinite depth of field, which, as Malkiewicz states, "doesn't allow for concentrating viewer's attention on important areas by selective focusing" (p. 192). Although shifting the focus on the large screen can direct the theatre audience's attention to important details, the same cannot be accomplished on video; a director must pan or zoom to the important visual element if he or she wants the audience to notice it. This results in increased camera movement.

Though these changes in filmmaking are present in today's movies, few successful Hollywood directors openly admit that they shoot their films with video release in mind. Robert Altman, however, steps forward to claim that directors must choose whether they film for the theatre or for the home video market: "If television is going to be a big part of the audience, if it's going to be important for you, then you should come as close as you can to using that frame – the square" (Oumano, 1985, p. 98). Another director, Martin Scorsese, welcomes video as an ally:

they [exhibitors] have to remember that something else is happening, that films are are being made directly for cable and cassette and this will increase. If they don't want to promote my films and put money into them, maybe I'll work with smaller budgets and make films only for cable. . . . the exhibitors shouldn't be threatened by cable and television – it will actually give them more product. (Oumano, p. 302)

These two attitudes suggest that some Hollywood directors are warming up to the video market.

Another indication of the warming trend is the increased use of video technology during film production. In filming One from the Heart, Francis Ford Coppola recorded technical rehearsals on video, so that he could review the visual elements immediately and alter composition before he did the actual shooting. This process, which he called "previsualization," not only turned directing into a more exact science but also saved Coppola money: "Applied to the entire script, this method was able to save millions of dollars in scenes that traditionally would have survived the shooting stage only to end up on the cutting-room floor" (Riley, 1982, p. 46). Moreover, Coppola continued his use of video technology in post-production; he developed a video playback system that allowed him to edit the film quickly and efficiently.

Another director who uses video technology in post-production is John G. Avildsen. Known for such films as Rocky, The Karate Kid, and Lean on Me, Avildsen freely admits his relationship with video: "I use the video editing in conjunction with the 35 mm film. I'm never concerned about the video being shown because the 35 mm film is cut to conform with what I've done on

---

Place words added for clarity in square brackets.

Use an ellipsis to indicate words omitted in a quotation.

video'' (Gallagher, 1989, p. 17). He further explains that video technology simplifies the otherwise complex process of filmmaking. His sentiments echo the warming attitude toward the use of video technology in the post-production stage of filmmaking.

While established directors are beginning to accept video as an ally, hungry new directors stake this medium as new territory that is ripe for exploitation. Instead of making feature films, these directors film their projects solely for release on video. To cut costs, they use 16 mm film rather than the conventional and more expensive 35 mm film; they also reduce costs by working with a skeleton crew, often doing much of the work themselves. The result has been phenomenal. One aspiring director, Roger Evans, produced a science-fiction comedy for under $6000; it grossed more than $130 000 in videocassette rentals. His next project, Forever Evil, was even more profitable:

> Thanks to the cost-cutting lessons learned by working in Super 8, Evans managed to deliver a finished film for under $120,000. Shot on 16 mm and distributed on home video, Forever Evil grossed over a million dollars in its first 90 days of release. (Frazier, 1989, pp. 79-80)

Evans and others are the new wave of directors who harvest video as a means of gaining success in Hollywood.

Though video will never replace film as an art form, it has forced Hollywood filmmakers to re-evaluate the way they make their movies. Technology has enhanced video so that it is as viable a market as the theatre; furthermore, video technology has crept into the production stages of filmmaking. Maverick directors depend on the market for their livelihood, while veteran filmmakers accept it as another medium through which to reach the masses. Ten years ago, Hollywood filmmakers would have cringed at the prospect of releasing their films on video; now they welcome it with open arms.

References

Brooks, J.L., & Greenhut, R. (Producers), & Marshall, P. (Director). (1988). Big [Film]. Twentieth-Century Fox.

Chute, D.(1984). Zapper power. Film Comment, 20, 49–56.

Cort, R.W., & Field, T. (Producers), & Nimoy, L. (Director). (1987). Three Men and a Baby [Film]. Touchstone.

Eidsvik, C. (1988). Machines of the invisible: Changes in film technology in the age of video. Film Quarterly, XL11, 18–23.

Finnell, M. (Producer), & Dante, J. (Director). (1987). Innerspace [Film]. Steven Spielberg, Kathleen Kennedy, and Frank Marshall.

Frazier, D. (1989). Big productions, small format. American Cinematographer, 70, 79–84.

Gallagher, J.A. (1989). [Interview with J.G. Avildsen]. In Film directors on directing (1–20). New York: Greenwood.

Malkiewicz, K. (1989). Cinematography. New York: Prentice-Hall.

Moffat, I. (Producer), & Stevens G. (Director). (1953). Shane [Film]. Paramount.

Oumano, E. (1985). Film forum: Thirty-five top filmmakers discuss their craft. New York: St. Martin's.

Riley, B. (1982). Film into video. Film Comment, 18, 45–48.

Schafer, R. (1986). Choice of transfers: Film to tape. American Cinematographer, 67, 97-103.

Strain, R.A. (1988). The shape of screens to come. Society of Motion Picture and Television Engineers Journal, 97, 560–67.

Wientraub, J. (Producer), & Avildsen, J.G. (Director). (1986). The Karate Kid, Part II [Film]. RCA/Columbia.

List references alphabetically by author's last name. Abbreviate first and second names to initials.

Note that all authors' names are reversed.

Ampersand is used in APA style.

See APA Reference Guide for headline style.

PART FIVE

Fit, Form, and Function

The Sentence Simplified

> Grammar is a piano I play by ear. All I know about grammar is its power.
>
> *Joan Didion*

Some fundamental understanding of the way a sentence is put together will help you analyze your style, eliminate grammatical errors, and punctuate more accurately. First, learn to differentiate the parts of a sentence.

When analyzing a sentence, always find the verb first. The verb is the part of the sentence that describes the action or the state of being. Next, find the subject: ask WHO or WHAT performed the action or is being described. Note that, usually, the subject appears before the verb.

Example

> *Dabney lost his nerve.*

What is the verb? (lost—an action)

What is the subject? *Who* or *what* lost his nerve? (Dabney)

> *His haircut looks dreadful.*

What is the verb? (looks—a state of being)

What is the subject? *Who* or *what* looks dreadful? (His haircut)

The most common English sentence is made up of a subject, a verb, and an object, usually in that order.

Example

> *Sweetiepie, the chimpanzee, refused to eat the banana.*
> S   V   O
>
> *It threw its food on the floor of the cage.*
> S V   O
>
> *It gave the zookeeper a nasty look.*
> S V   O

Even chimpanzees lose their temper.
    S   V   O

In each of these cases, the first noun or pronoun in the sentence is the subject, which performs the action. What follows the subject is the predicate, made up of the verb, which describes the action, and the object, which receives the action.

Another common simple sentence pattern is subject, verb, and complement, sometimes called a "subjective completion." Here the verb must be a linking verb that describes a state of being, rather than an action.

Example

Mary Jane is not a good dancer.
   S   V   C

She often seems clumsy.
 S   V   C

She appears unaware of her partner's dismay.
 S   V   C

Some people just don't look graceful.
  S   V   C

A sentence is a grammatical unit that can stand alone. It must be composed of a subject and verb and is usually accompanied by an object or a complement.

■ Parts of Speech

A knowledge of the roles parts of speech play will help you understand how your sentences are constructed.

Nouns

Nouns name something, a person, place, or thing. They may be abstract or concrete. As a general rule, something may be classified as a noun if you can put an article ("a," "an," or "the") or a possessive pronoun ("my," "her") in front of it.

Example

advertising	corset
philosophy	computer
doctor	giraffe

Pronouns

Pronouns stand in the place of nouns. There are many kinds of pronouns.

Personal: I, you, he, she, we, they (subjective)
             me, you, him, her, us, them (objective)

my, your, his, her, our, their (possessive)

mine, yours, his, hers, ours, theirs (absolute possessive)

*I never should have lent **her my** new flashlight.*

Reflexive or **Intensive**: myself, yourself, and so on

*Frankenstein's creature was shocked when he looked at **himself** in the mirror.* (reflective)

*I did it all by **myself**.* (intensive)

Relative: who, which, that, whose, whoever, whomever, whichever, and so on

*The best friends are those **who** know when to keep quiet.*

These pronouns connect subordinate clauses to main clauses.

Interrogative: who, whom, which, what

***What** do you mean by that?*

These pronouns begin questions.

Demonstrative: this, that, these, those, such

***Such** is life.*

These pronouns point to someone or something.

Indefinite: any, some, each, every, few, everyone, everybody, someone, somebody

***Everybody** loves **somebody** sometime.*

These pronouns stand for an indefinite number of people or things.

Reciprocal: each other, one another

*Scott and Zelda hated **each other** intensely.*

These pronouns express a reciprocal relationship.

Verbs

A verb is an action word or a word that describes a state of being. It may have many forms and tenses. It also may be composed of an auxiliary verb and a main verb. Verbs may be transitive or intransitive (some verbs may be either), or linking.

A transitive verb needs an object to be complete.

*Winston **shut** his mouth.*

An intransitive verb is complete without an object.

*Rita **yawned**.*

A linking verb connects the subject to a state of being.

*Malcolm **is** mischievous.*

Adjectives

Adjectives describe or modify nouns.

Examples

delicious	wooden
handsome	abstract
devilish	superstitious

Adverbs

Adverbs describe or modify verbs, adjectives, and other adverbs. They often end in "ly."

soon	too
devilishly	now
often	generally

Prepositions
The preposition is a linking word that is always followed by a noun.

Examples

on the wagon	according to her
in your mind	by all accounts
to the lifeboats	from me to you

Conjunctions
Conjunctions are used to join two words, phrases, or clauses.

Examples

The office sent invoices to those **who** owed money **and** greeting cards to those **who** did not.
After the war was over, Ashley returned to Melanie.
Love is **as** strong **as** death.

Interjections
Interjections are exclamatory words or phrases that interrupt a sentence.

Examples

No, I don't want to go to the dentist.
My word! I simply don't believe what you say.

NOTE: Keep the following definitions in mind as you read the next chapter.

Phrase
A phrase is a group of words.

Examples

playing doctor
in the tree house

Clause
A group of words with a subject and a verb.

Examples

We were playing doctor in the tree house.

Common Sentence Problems

> — All those clauses, appositions, amplifications, qualifications, asides, God knows what else, hanging inside the poor old skeleton of one sentence like some kind of Spanish moss.
> *Tom Wolfe*

A well-structured sentence tells its readers where to start and where to stop. The sentence, if it is correctly formed, constitutes a complete thought. It contains a main subject and a main verb connected to the subject.

■ Sentence Structure

Avoid fragments

A sentence fragment lacks either a subject or a main verb. Or, sometimes, it ignores the connection between them.

Example

X *Ramona did not follow the cheesecake recipe. But added Cheddar instead of cream cheese.*

(missing subject: she)

✔ *Ramona did not follow the cheesecake recipe. She added Cheddar instead of cream cheese.*
X *Wilhelm enjoyed many forms of relaxation. Practising tai chi, doing origami, and baking cookies.*

(no connection to the subject: he)

✔ *Wilhelm enjoyed many forms of relaxation: practising tai chi, doing origami, and baking cookies.*
X *Norrie didn't bring his homework. Because Fido ate it.*
✔ *Norrie didn't bring his homework because Fido ate it.*

NOTE: A fragment may, on rare occasions, be used for rhetorical effect. Deliberate fragments must, however, be used sparingly. It is also a wise idea to use a dash (two hyphens in typing) before a deliberate sentence fragment to indicate its purpose to your reader.

Example

Should colleges and universities have the right to charge foreign students higher tuition than native-born students? — Under no circumstances.

Avoid run-on sentences

A run-on sentence is actually two sentences that run together without any punctuation to indicate where one ends and the next begins.

Example

X *Hedda couldn't sleep on the new waterbed she always felt seasick.*
✔ *Hedda couldn't sleep on the new waterbed. She always felt seasick.*

Avoid comma splices

A comma splice is similar to a run-on sentence. It occurs when two main clauses are "spliced," or incorrectly joined, by a comma. The comma splice fails to show the relationship between two clauses.

Example

X *Graeme had too much to drink, he got the hiccups.*
X *His mother was the designated driver, she took him home.*

A comma splice, like a visible seam, is a sign of faulty workmanship. There are several methods by which it may be corrected. Run-ons may also be treated the same way:

1. Join the two ideas with one of the following co-ordinating conjunctions: and, or, nor, for, but, yet, so.

Example

✔ *Graeme had too much to drink, and he got the hiccups.*
✔ *His mother was the designated driver, so she took him home.*

2. Join the two ideas with a subordinating conjunction.

Example

✔ *Because Graeme had too much to drink, he got the hiccups.*
✔ *Since his mother was the designated driver, she took him home.*

3. Form two separate sentences.

Example

✔ *Graeme had too much to drink. He got the hiccups.*
✔ *His mother was the designated driver. She took him home.*

4. Join the two ideas with a semicolon.

Use this method of correction only if the two ideas in question are logically connected. Note that sometimes a word may be used as a conjunctive adverb to join two sentences with a semicolon. Such words as "however," "therefore," and "hence" frequently serve this function. For more information, see page 111.

Example

    ✔ *Graeme had too much to drink; he got the hiccups.*
    ✔ *His mother was the designated driver; she took him home.*

EXERCISE

Correct run-ons, fragments, and comma splices in the following sentences. Some may be correct as they stand.

1. When he visited other people's houses, Patrick's bad habits included picking lint off the furniture and straightening the pictures on the wall.
2. Flossing your teeth is important I grant you that however I usually keep my teeth in a glass by the bed.
3. I don't think our dinner guest likes cats he sneezed twice in the last two minutes and furthermore he just asked Boots in an undertone if she thought there was enough room in the closet to swing a cat.
4. Horace sent greeting cards to all his enemies and presents to all his relatives his behaviour demonstrates the triumph of niceness, if not of good will.
5. Being one of those people who have always handed papers in on time.
6. When Godfrey tries on shorts, he always jumps up and down in the changing room if anything jiggles, he settles for long pants.
7. When Fred's mother came to visit his new apartment, she conducted long inspections. Often standing on the kitchen counter checking the cupboards for ants and cockroaches.
8. Jack contended that swimsuit competitions were sexist he suggested that the judges should test the poise and grace of the competitors by outfitting them with lumberjack jackets and steel-toed boots, those still looking self-assured would win.
9. Douglas and Mary were bored with home renovations still they thought perhaps they should replace the doorknob on the bathroom.
10. Howard was delighted with his horoscope today rather than going to work, he was going to have an appointment with destiny.

■ Modifiers

Modifiers are descriptive words or phrases. A modifier may be a simple adverb or an adjective, or a more complex adverbial phrase or adjectival phrase. A modifier should describe clearly and unambiguously. To do so, it must be as near in the sentence as possible to the thing described.

Avoid misplaced modifiers

    A modifier, whether a word or a phrase, should be placed next to the word it describes.

Examples

    X *Emmylou chased the mouse carrying a knife.*

✔ *Carrying a knife, Emmylou chased the mouse.*
X *Licking each other fondly, the children admired the kittens.*
✔ *Licking each other fondly, the kittens were admired by the children.*

Watch the position of limiting modifiers

A limiting modifier is a word that qualifies part or all of the statement. Consider carefully the placement of the following modifiers (and others): only, just, nearly, almost, hardly.

Examples

Only Gilbert brought a case of beer.

(No one else brought one.)

Gilbert brought only a case of beer.

(He brought only one case.)

Gilbert brought a case of beer only.

(He didn't bring a case of wine.)

Avoid squinting modifiers

A squinting modifier is ambiguously placed in the sentence, so that the writer's intention is unclear.

Examples

*The suspect confessed that he had served time **later**.*
*The suspect confessed **later** that he had served time.*

Avoid dangling modifiers

A modifier dangles when what it is meant to describe is accidentally left out of the sentence. To figure out what it does describe, ask WHO or WHAT is being described.

Examples

X *After vacuuming the living-room rug, the cat tracked mud all over it.*
✔ *After vacuuming the living-room rug, I saw that the cat had tracked mud all over it.*

OR

✔ *After I vacuumed the living-room rug, the cat tracked mud all over it.*

Dangling modifiers that end in "ing" are usually easy to spot. Remember, however, that a dangling modifier may also involve a prepositional phrase or an infinitive form. A dangling modifier may also occur at the end of a sentence.

Examples

X *As a weightlifter, my muscles are in tremendous shape.*
✔ *As a weightlifter, I believe that my muscles are in tremendous shape.*
X *To get a high-paying job, education is essential.*

✔ To get a high-paying job, you need education.
✗ Fernando's travel bills were expensive, being used to flying first class.
✔ Being used to flying first class, Fernando had expensive travel bills.

OR

✔ Since Fernando was used to flying first class, his travel bills were expensive.

Note that some modifiers apply to the entire sentence rather than to any one word or phrase within it. These constructions, called "absolute modifiers," include phrases such as "To make a long story short" and "All things considered."

EXERCISE

Correct the modifier problems in the following sentences.
1. Cherries are enjoyed by many fruit lovers, especially when covered in chocolate.
2. After clawing the couch to shreds, the maid sent the cat from the living room.
3. After defrosting overnight, the chef prepared the filet mignon.
4. Just like you, my work comes first.
5. Raoul read that true love was always rewarded in a romance novel.
6. Having failed obedience school, the owners of the basset hound scolded him.
7. After spending all day in a ten-hectare shopping mall, not one Christmas present was purchased by Cathy.
8. Being hungry most of the time, ice cream doesn't last long in my refrigerator.
9. Fascinated, the spiders in the pet store were observed by the kindergarten class.
10. Why do they only criticize me?

■ Pronoun Reference and Agreement

A pronoun, as the name suggests, acts for a noun, or in the place of a noun. A pronoun should almost always refer to a specific noun in the sentence itself. The noun to which it refers is called an "antecedent." When a pronoun does not refer clearly to its antecedent, confusing or ambiguous writing is the result.

A guide to proper pronoun usage

Make sure your pronoun matches its antecedent. A pronoun must agree in gender: it may be masculine (he, him, his), feminine (she, her, hers), or neuter (it, it, its). A pronoun must also agree in number: it may be singular or plural.

In gender

Examples

Nancy named **her** dachshund Simon.
Nancy named **him** Simon.

In the second sentence, "her dachshund" has been replaced by the masculine pronoun "him."

In the past, the masculine pronouns ("he," "his," "him") were used to refer generally to nouns that were not specifically feminine.

Example

*The reader must make up **his** own mind.*

Although the masculine pronoun is still, strictly speaking, grammatically correct, many people now find its general use offensive. It is now more common to find such cases phrased as

*The reader must make up **his or her** own mind.*

For those tho find the use of "his or her" cumbersome, the best solution is to use the plural pronoun and an accompanying plural noun, of course.

Example

*Readers must make up **their** own minds.*

The determination of gender in English does not pose much of a problem, apart from this dispute. Problems do arise, however, with the number of pronouns.

In number

1. Be sure to locate the correct antecedent for the pronoun in question.

Example

*Chloë is one of those students **who** skip their classes regularly.*

"Students is the antecedent of the relative pronoun WHO. Both the verb "skip" and the pronoun "their" are plural. Note that "one of those" takes the plural, but "one of these" is singular. One of these gloves is lost.

2. Be especially careful with collective nouns and their pronoun replacements.

When a collective noun is considered as a unit, the pronoun that stands for it is singular.

Example

*The jury **has** reached an impasse.*

Here the jury acts as a unit.

When the component parts of a collective noun are considered individually, the pronoun that stands for it is plural.

Example

*The jury **have** been unable to agree.*

Here the jury acts individually; each member has his or her own opinion.

3. Be careful of imprecise use of some indefinite pronouns.

"Anyone," "anybody," "someone," "somebody," "everyone," "everybody," "each," "either," "neither," "nobody," and "no one" are indefinite pronouns, all of which generally take singular verbs.

Example
_____

Nobody wore his or her bathing suit.

Ideally, "his or her" should allow an indefinite pronoun, if the construction is to avoid charges of sexism. In conversation, many people would get around this problem by saying,

Nobody wore their bathing suits.

This form, despite its regular occurrence in spoken English, is still considered imprecise grammatically. It should properly be replaced by the following:

None of us wore our bathing suits.

The best approach is to use the plural form.

In case

Pronouns, besides being masculine or feminine, singular or plural, also have different forms depending on their case. They may be used as subjects ("he," "she," "they"), objects ("him," "her," "them"), or possessives ("his," "her," "their").

1. Use the subjective form if the pronoun is the subject of a verb (stated or implied).

Example
_____

*The police officer stated that it was **she** who had reported the theft of the painting.*

"She" is used here because a verb is implied.

*It was **they** who had masterminded the heist.*

"They" and not "them" is used here because it functions as the subject of the verb "had masterminded."

This precision is essential in writing English, but in informal speech, by contrast, "It's me" or "It was her" are considered acceptable.

2. Make sure to use the objective form of the pronoun if it is the object of a verb.

Example
_____

The poodle gave his master fleas.
*The poodle gave **him them**.*

In the second version, the objective forms for both pronouns—objects of the verb "gave"—have been substituted.

> The poodle gave **his master and me** fleas.

Although you might be tempted to write "The poodle gave his master and I fleas," it becomes obvious that the objective pronoun "me" is correct when you remove the words "his master and." When the pronoun case is a problem, try taking out part of a compound subject and reading the sentence. The correct pronoun should then be obvious.

3. **Make sure to use the objective form of the pronoun if it is the object of a preposition.**

Example

> Between **you** and **me**, I think you should use deodorant.
> It's important for **you** and **me** to wear clean underwear every day.

4. **After "than" or "as," use the form of the pronoun that would be required in the complete implied clause.**

Examples

> A sloth is harder working than **he** [is].
> A monkey can communicate as well as **she** [can].

Note the difference in meaning in the following examples:

> I love you as much as **he** [does].
> I love you as much as [I love] **him**.

■ Pronoun Problems in Essay Writing

Use personal pronouns with discretion

Too few personal references in an essay may be as awkward as too many. Few instructors disallow the use of "I" entirely. Its occasional use should prevent needless circumlocution and impersonality. Never stoop to cold and formal constructions like "It is the opinion of this writer," or the overly polite "myself." "We" is sometimes acceptable, though its overuse may sound pompous. "One" may serve as an alternative, though it runs the risk of sounding too distanced and impersonal.

You are writing your paper: its words and thoughts are yours. Avoid "I" and "in my opinion" only when a personal perspective might make your point seem weak or merely a matter of personal idiosyncrasy.

Check to see that your pronoun references are present and accounted for

> UNCLEAR: In small towns, they do not lock their cars.
> CLEARER: Residents of small towns do not lock their cars.
> UNCLEAR: Esther changed the baby's diaper, and it screamed.
> CLEARER: When Esther changed its diaper, the baby screamed.
> UNCLEAR: Robert hates studying floristry, but he intends to become one anyway.
> CLEARER: Robert hates studying floristry, but he intends to become a florist anyway.

Avoid broad pronoun references

A broad pronoun reference occurs when "this," "which," or "that" is used to refer to an idea rather than to a specific word in the sentence. Some broad references may be tolerated, if the meaning is generally clear. Be careful of raising unanswered questions in the reader's mind, however.

> UNCLEAR: Dexter stays up all night watching reruns of "Leave It to Beaver," which is why he falls asleep on the job so often.
> CLEARER: Dexter stays up all night watching reruns of "Leave It to Beaver," a habit which causes him to fall asleep on the job often.

"Which" does not clearly refer to any specific noun in the preceding sentence. Add a noun before "which" to clarify the point.

EXERCISE

Improve the usage of the pronouns in the following sentences:
1. If either him or her objects to sleeping on the floor, you could flip a coin to see whether they get to sleep in the bathtub.
2. "What I do with my investments," said his grandmother, "is up to my stockbroker and I."
3. If a customer is not pleased with their meal, they should first check to see if he got what he ordered.
4. Although Diana is taller than him, her flat heels put both Charles and she on the same level.
5. In this self-help book, it says that everyone can raise their I.Q. and their salary.
6. Alison pulled the donkey's tail, and it kicked her.
7. Allan bought some old clothes from Goodwill just like her.
8. Each of the drivers illegally parked in the handicapped zone was upset by their parking ticket and by the nails in their tires.
9. People like you and him whom own fur coats should ask themselves if they are as conscious of wildlife preservation as we.
10. To take an interest in butterfly collecting, you don't have to be one.

■ Subject and Verb Agreement

The subject and verb in a sentence are closely connected. In order for the sentence to express itself clearly, the subject and the verb must agree.

Most problems with agreement between subject and verb result from difficulties in locating the subject of a verb. Solve these problems by locating the verb in each clause. Remember, first, that a verb describes either an action or a state of being. Next, ask WHO or WHAT is performing that action or is being described. The answer to the question WHO or WHAT is the subject of the verb. Having located the subject and verb, you may then check to see that they match.

Example

> Big Brother is watching you.

WHO is watching?
— Big Brother (the subject of the verb "is watching")

How to match subjects and verbs correctly

Check to see that verbs agree in number with their subjects. In other words, singular subjects take singular verbs; plural subjects take plural verbs.

Problems to watch for:

1. The noun that immediately precedes the verb may not be the subject.

Example

> Not one of these science-fiction writers has ever seen an extra-terrestrial creature.

The correct subject is "one."

2. Subjects joined by "and" are usually, but not always, plural.

Example

> My friend and guardian angel has come to my rescue.

"My friend and guardian angel" refers to one person.

3. Singular subjects that are joined by a phrase other than "and" are not made plural. Such phrases as "as well as," "in addition to," and "along with" have no effect on the agreement of the verb since they are not part of the subject.

Example

> A hamburger, along with french fries, is Dee's typical dinner.

"Along with french fries" is not part of the subject.

4. Subjects joined by "or" or "nor" are each considered separately. The verb agrees with the subject closest to it.

Example

> Neither tears nor litigation moves Scrooge to act fairly toward his employees.

"Tears" and "litigation" are each considered separately; since "litigation" is closer, the verb is singular.

5. The following subjects always take singular verbs: "each," "either," "neither," "one," and words ending in "body" or "one."

Example

> Neither of the twins eats turnip.

6. **Subjects like "some," "all," "most," "any," or "none" may take singular or plural verbs depending upon the noun to which they refer.**

Examples

Some of the guests refuse to eat parsnip.
All of us enjoy caviar.

(plural verb)

All of the caviar is gone.

(singular verb)

7. **A collective noun, used to refer to a group of people or things, takes a singular verb when the collective is considered as a unit and a plural verb when each member is considered individually.**

Example

Singular (considered a unit): *The union is planning a strike.*

Plural (considered as individuals within the group): *The union are voting on the new benefits package.*

8. **A linking verb (a verb describing a state of being) agrees with its subject and not with its predicate.**

Example

The only thing Myrna ever buys is cigarettes.

"Thing" is the subject; hence, "is" is the appropriate verb.

OR

Cigarettes are the only thing Myrna ever buys.

In this example, "cigarettes" is the subject; hence, the plural verb is correct.

9. **A verb still agrees with its subject, even when their order is inverted. The subject follows "there is" or "there are," "here is" or "here are," and the verb is singular or plural accordingly.**

Example

Here are the pizzas you ordered.

Here "pizzas" is the subject; hence, the correct verb is "are."

10. **Relative pronouns (who, which, that), acting as subjects, take singular or plural verbs depending on the words to which they refer (their antecedents).**

Example

Harry is one of those people who cheat at Scrabble.

"People," the antecedent of "who," is plural; hence, the verb "cheat" is also plural.

BUT NOTE:

Harry is the only one of us who spells badly.

"One" is the antecedent in this case; hence, the verb "spells" is singular.

11. Some nouns may look plural though they are actually singular. Examples. includes "physics," "economics," "ethics," and "news." Check doubtful usage in a dictionary.

Example

News is big business on television today.

EXERCISE

Correct the alignments between subject and verb in the following sentences.

1. Neither the escalator nor the glass elevator are safe for one of those people who is scared of heights.
2. Grinding your teeth, as well as suffering from the hiccups, are not appropriate behaviour at the table.
3. Here lies my pet squirrel, Trixie, and my pet hamster, Roderick.
4. At the back of the airplane, which looked like a bus with wings, was a small washroom and the emergency exit.
5. Every one of these advertisements for mouthwash claim to combat dental plaque as well as bad breath.
6. He, in addition to his brother, feel like part of a SWAT team whenever they baby-sit their sister Rosie.
7. The risk of accidents when using a corkscrew to open a bottle of wine are not high.
8. Behind the small cottage was a beautiful deserted forest and a privy with a chemical toilet.
9. The subject of both the ballet *Giselle* and *The Life and Loves of a She-Devil* are revenge.
10. The mass media is often held responsible for encouraging people to engage in acts of greed and violence.

■ End Punctuation

1. Use a period after a statement, an indirect question, or a command.

Examples

I have something to tell you. (statement)

Don't look now. (command)

Penny asked me when I got my nose fixed. (indirect question)

2. Use a period after most abbreviations, unless they are easily recognized. Note that some formal abbreviations, such as Mr., Mrs., and Dr., always end with a period in common usage.

Examples

Mr.	*CBC*
Mrs.	*VCR*
Dr.	*CD player*

3. Use a question mark after a direct question.

Examples

Who's been eating my porridge?
Whatever is the matter?
What's for supper?

4. Use exclamation marks sparingly to express emphasis, in an informal essay. Use them in a formal essay at your own risk.

Example

X Hugo did his homework!
✔ Amazingly, Hugo did his homework.

■ The Colon

The colon (:) is used to introduce something. Remember the following rules for colon usage:

1. Use a colon only after a complete sentence (that is, after an independent clause).

Example

X Delores loved: foreign vacations, fur coats, and cold cash.
✔ Delores loved three things: foreign vacations, fur coats, and cold cash.

2. Use a colon after a complete sentence to introduce ideas, lists, or quotations.

Examples

Lucy van Pelz wants only one thing for Christmas: real estate.
Bette Midler makes this claim: "The worst part of success is to try finding someone who is happy for you."

3. Use a colon to indicate amplification or further development of an idea.

Example

Thanatology is a branch of psychology: it deals with the subject of death and dying.

■ The Semicolon

A semicolon (;) is a heavier punctuation mark than a comma, but lighter than a period. Use a semicolon generally only where you might use a period instead.

Semicolons are especially useful in the following cases:

1. Use a semicolon to join two closely related main clauses.

The use of a semicolon instead of a co-ordinating conjunction shows a close connection (or a sharp antithesis) between two ideas.

Example

Man proposes; God disposes.

2. Use a semicolon with a transitional word or phrase when it is used to join two main clauses.

Transitional words or phrases such as "however," "moreover," "furthermore," "hence," "as a result," and "consequently" may be used in this way.

Example

I won't accept charity; however, I will take cash or travellers' cheques.

The semicolon takes the place of a period in this sentence.

BUT NOTE:

I will not, however, accept charity.

In this case, "however" is not used to join two main clauses. Since the transitional word interrupts one main clause, commas are adequate punctuation.

3. Use a semicolon to separate items listed in a series, if commas are already used as internal punctuation.

Example

Maxwell always did three things before he went to bed: one, he put on his pyjamas; two, he drank warm milk; three, he fell asleep in the armchair in front of the TV set.

EXERCISE

Add or substitute colons or semicolons in the following sentences, keeping in mind that some may be correct as they stand.
1. Mary Anne needed a painting over the fireplace Kim offered to paint portraits of her friends as Disney characters.
2. Monika has never liked most popular music however she does admire Simon, Alvin, and Theodore.
3. If the building were burning down, Benny would save one person the employee who signs his paycheque every week.

4. Never forget the simple rules of etiquette don't talk with your mouth full, don't say insulting things about anyone's pets or children, however much such insults may be deserved, and leave parties before the hosts fall asleep.
5. On good days, Kerry planned to buy a sports car on bad days, he saved his pennies to buy a new bicycle.
6. He requested a Tilley hat, some safari shorts, and a Swiss army knife for his birthday nevertheless his ideas of the great outdoors usually came from *National Geographic*.
7. Dying one's hair can be a delightful experience you do not however want to glow in the dark.
8. The couple wondered what to call the twins Laverne and Shirley Daisy and Donald or Calvin and Hobbes.
9. There is one disadvantage to owning a lap-top computer you can take your work with you even though you may not want to.
10. Grammar books are pompous, boring, and confusing.

◼ The Comma

A comma (,) is a light mark of punctuation. Some basic rules that govern its use are listed below. When in doubt about a particular usage, let ease in reading be your guide.

1. Use a comma before "and," "or," "nor," "for," "but," "yet," "so," if any of these words are used to join two independent clauses.

Example

Gunther doesn't normally snore, but tonight his dog needs earplugs.

BUT NOTE:
A comma should not be used if a complete independent clause does not follow.

Example

Ivor hates school but loves recess.

In this case, "but" actually joins a compound verb, rather than two independent clauses.

2. You may use a comma after a word, a phrase, or a clause used to introduce the main subject and verb. The comma is essential if the sentence would be confusing without it.

Examples

Bracing himself, Rocky applied for a job as a snake charmer.
Because he had never seen a snake before, Rocky was different from the other candidates.
Alas, the snake did not find him charming enough.

3. Use a comma after a word or phrase that modifies an entire sentence. To find out whether something is a sentence modifier, test to see if it can be moved elsewhere in the sentence without changing the meaning.

Example

> *However, he did find work cleaning cages at the zoo.*

"However" can be shifted in the sentence; hence, it is a sentence modifier.

> *He did, however, find work cleaning cages at the zoo.*

4. Use a comma for the sake of contrast before an antithetical element.

Examples

> *Tracy attended school for the social life, not for the good of her mind.*
> *Pee-Wee wanted precious antiques, but found worthless junk.*

5. Use commas to separate elements in a series.

Examples

> *Cinderella invited Flora, Fauna, and Merryweather to her coming-out party.*

A comma before "and" at the end of the list is usually advisable to prevent confusion.

> *Ogden told us that his old age had begun, and his middle age had ended, and now his descendants outnumbered his friends.*

Here a comma is used to separate a series of independent clauses. Note, however, that two independent clauses together must normally be separated by a semicolon.

6. Put commas around words, phrases, or clauses that interrupt a sentence. Commas may be used around a word or a group of words if that part of the sentence might be removed and still leave a subject and predicate.

Examples

> *Bram loves children, especially when they cry, for then someone takes them away.*
> *Yes, Virginia, there is a Santa Claus.*

7. Put commas around appositives, words that rename those that precede.

Examples

> *Jethro and Elly May, Melissa's pet gerbils, are on the loose again.*
> *Madame de Pompadour said that Canada, then a colony of France, was only useful to provide her with furs.*

8. Put commas around interrupting phrases or clauses that are non-restrictive in meaning.

Examples

> *My grandmother, who lives in Los Angeles, is getting a divorce.*

Here the clause "who lives in Los Angeles" is non-restrictive, and it implies that the author has one grandmother; some incidental information about her is enclosed in commas.

BUT NOTE:

> *My grandmother who lives in Los Angeles is getting a divorce.*

Here the clause "who lives in Los Angeles" is restrictive and lacks commas. It implies that the author has two grandmothers and uses the clause to identify which one.

9. **Commas should not enclose material that is restrictive, that is, essential to the sentence's meaning.**

Example

> X *People, who live in glass houses, shouldn't throw stones.*

This sentence, because of the way it is punctuated, says that all people shouldn't throw stones.

> ✔ *People who live in glass houses shouldn't throw stones.*

This statement identifies those people who shouldn't throw stones. The modifier, because it performs the necessary function of identification or limitation, cannot be surrounded by commas.

10. **Commas should not separate main sentence elements. Do not use a comma between a subject and verb or between a verb and an object or complement.**

Example

> X *Everything Zsa Zsa does, gets on my nerves.*
> ✔ *Everything Zsa Zsa does gets on my nerves.*

EXERCISE

Add commas, or other punctuation, where needed in the following sentences:

1. Ernie's best friends Soph and Clementine were known for their wit charm and tendency to say rude and slanderous things.
2. Yoko's favourite line in Cecil B. de Mille's epic movie *The Ten Commandments* was "Moses Moses you mad silly impetuous fool" she wondered how either Charlton Heston or Anne Baxter ever managed to keep a straight face.
3. Whenever Wendy walked through the shopping mall with her children Chester and Lester she felt as though they were training her for the 4:40 yet somehow she had never thought of shopping as aerobic exercise.
4. Paul's advice to the tourists was simple but powerful keep the wagons in a circle and don't let the bears hear your knees knocking together.
5. Think twice about buying any book that costs $40 that is after all the price of two cases of beer and we all must have our priorities.
6. Woody Allen her favourite film director admits that he likes to think of himself as God because as he says he has to model himself after somebody.

7. Gerry objected to the cottage for it lacked two essentials a warm place to sleep and an indoor toilet.

8. Through wind and rain and sleet and snow Lorna could hear Phillip's voice still echoing his most often repeated question "Where are your gloves?"

9. At every high-level conference Norbert had ever attended were two things a lot of people who tried in vain to impress each other and a banquet at which for some reason a rubber chicken was almost always the main course.

10. I have the highest regard for your feelings said Mr. Bennett however I do have some reservations I'm afraid about your intellect.

■ The Dash

Type a dash using two hyphens, with no spaces before or after.

Example

I won't drink--I want to know when I'm having a good time.

1. Use a dash for emphasis around parenthetical expressions.

Example

The show--though a huge success with the public--was panned by the critics.

Note: Commas are also correct in this sentence, but less emphatic.

2. Use a dash to introduce something with extra emphasis.

Example

Rob loved birthday cards--whether cheques were enclosed or not.

Note: A colon is also correct in this sentence but less emphatic.

3. Keep the dash in reserve for special occasions. Use it sparingly, especially in formal writing.

■ Parentheses

Parentheses are used to enclose incidental material. They (that is, the words they enclose) serve the same function as an aside in a theatrical production. Though they get the reader's attention, the material they enclose is presented as "inside information."

1. Use parentheses in formal writing to enclose the necessary definition of a term at its first appearance.

Example

The NFB (National Film Board of Canada) has won several Academy Awards for its productions.

2. Use parentheses to enclose any part of a sentence that might be enclosed by commas or dashes, if the reader has only passing interest in it.

Example

In the next episode of "Degrassi Junior High" (Saturday night at nine), the twins seek a cure for acne.

3. **Use parentheses sparingly. Too many make the writing self-conscious and hard to follow.**

Example

X In this report (which is the product of months of arduous research), I will discuss various methods of sleep-teaching.

Possession

Apostrophes are used after nouns and indefinite pronouns (e.g., "anyone," "somebody") to indicate possession. Note these general rules:

1. **Add " 's" to form the possessive case if the owner is singular.**

Examples

monkey's uncle-the uncle of the monkey

horse's mouth-the mouth of the horse

pig's eye-the eye of the pig

Note that even when the word ends in "s," the ending is usually " 's," since that is how we pronounce it.

Examples

James's novels-the novels of James

Stevens's poetry-the poetry of Stevens

2. **Add "s' " to the form of the possessive case if the owners are plural.**

Examples

workers' coalition-the coalition of workers

boys' team-the team of boys

But note that words that do not form the plural with "s" are made possessive by the addition of " 's."

Examples

women's rights-the rights of women

people's court-the court of people

men's washroom-the washroom of men

3. **Do not use an apostrophe with possessive pronouns.**

Example

The villa is his, the Mercedes is hers, and the Swiss bank account is theirs.

Note that "its" (another possessive pronoun) also does not have an apostrophe. Do not confuse the possessive pronoun "its" with the contraction for "it is."

Examples

It's time to take you home. (It is time)

Its diaper wet, the baby fussed noisily. (possessive case)

EXERCISE

Correct the following sentences by adding apostrophes where necessary.
1. For dinner at the Smiths house we have Eloises world-class kidneys and giblets.
2. In three days time, the effects of the allergy shots will wear off, and Timmys sinuses will bother him so much that he will no longer be able to tolerate the bunnies as pets.
3. Dieter hated lawn ornaments though one of his friends sisters, Carmen, bought him Santas reindeer and carried them through the United States customs on the roof of her car.
4. Jackie loved to watch "Peoples Court" after a hard days work, but the new seasons afternoon programming, featuring Road Runner cartoons, suited her childrens tastes better than hers.
5. Cathys new dog, Electra, and her friends baby, Zenith, are two of the comic strips funniest characters.
6. For Petes sake, stop behaving like the cats meow, and try to get a good nights sleep.
7. At McDonalds, the foods taste and textures are always consistent, but the boys tastebuds incline them toward their mothers home cooking.
8. Donalds aunt loved Hopkins poetry, Dickens novels, and Sears catalogues.
9. When one of her cheques bounced, Maryanne thought she recognized the bank managers face as one she had seen on a wanted poster, and she made a citizens arrest.
10. Guys favourite flavours were Seagrams Special Blend, Labatts Classic, and Molsons Canadian.

Elements of Style: Structuring the Sentences

> Style is the dress of thought, and a well-dressed thought, like a well-dressed man, appears to great advantage.
>
> *Earl of Chesterfield*

V ariety in your sentence structure will ensure that your reader pays attention, not only to what you say, but also to the way you say it. Try to develop an awareness of the subtle changes in emphasis and reading pace that occur when you modify the structure of a sentence. Such consciousness will enhance your style and impress your reader.

■ Sentence Variation

1.   **Vary your sentence structure.**

The following are examples of different types of sentences.

Simple Sentence—one independent clause

Donald and Ivana split their assets equitably in the divorce settlement.

Compound Sentence—two independent clauses joined by one of the co-ordinating conjunctions (and, or, nor, for, but, yet, so)

Donald kept his business empire, and Ivana kept her wardrobe and her cosmetics.

Complex Sentence—one independent clause joined to one dependent clause

Marriage is a lottery in which couples stake their happiness and their worldly goods.

Note: Dependent clauses begin with a subordinating conjunction, such as one of the following:

after	because	however	that
although	before	if	though
as	how	since	

Subordinate, or dependent, clauses also begin with words starting with a "wh–"—when, where, why, which, who, while, whereas, what—except where these words introduce questions.

Compounds-Complex Sentence—a compound sentence joined to a complex sentence

> *They knew that a lot of people didn't expect their marriage to last, so they celebrated their first anniversary six months early.*

2.   **Practise subordination by converting groups of simple or compound sentences you find in your writing into complex sentences.**

Example

> *The patient in the clinic asked a question. Why is it that we talk to God, and we call it praying. God talks to us, and doctors call it schizophrenia.*
>
> REVISED: *The patient in the clinic asked why when we talk to God, we call it praying, whereas when God talks to us, doctors call it schizophrenia.*

3.   **Practice joining simple sentences together using verbal phrases rather than subordinators. Start by changing the verb into a participle (usually ending in "ing" or "ed"). Then remove its subject, and connect it to the appropriate word in the following sentence.**

Example

> *Joshua stayed in bed this morning. He is suffering from a hangover.*
>
> REVISED: *Suffering from a hangover, Joshua stayed in bed this morning.*

4.   **Practice cutting tangled constructions down to size by using simple sentences where the reader might have difficulty in understanding or where you wish to place more emphasis.**

Example

> *A factory job is superior to a job requiring post-secondary education. Some would argue the opposite. Still, the advantages of a factory job are numerous. Here are some of these advantages. A factory worker makes more money at an earlier age than a college student. Thus he can live on his own earlier. A factory worker also has more spare time to pursue other goals. There is also less stress placed on a factory worker. He is more likely to be happy and healthy.*
>
> REVISED: *Although some would argue the opposite, a factory job is superior to a job requiring post-secondary education. Because a factory worker makes more money at an earlier age than a college student, he is able to live on his own earlier. In addition, because a factory worker has more time to pursue other goals and faces less stress than someone in a white-collar job, he is more likely to be happy and healthy.*

5.   **Try converting some of the phrases and dependent clauses in your writing into absolutes (phrases with connecting words removed). Keep the subject of the clause and its accompanying participle; remove other words.**

Example

> *Because his tire was flat and his hopes of winning races were gone, Mario decided to become a gas-station attendant.*

REVISED: *His tire flat and his hopes of winning races gone, Mario decided to become a gas-station attendant.*

6. **Vary your sentences by making them more suspenseful. The typical English sentence moves directly from subject to verb to object or complement, a structure often called "loose." In other languages, the word order is often not so direct, placing subject or verb near the end of the sentence. This structure is called "periodic." Try making your own sentences periodic occasionally, so that the impact of the thought is delayed.**

Examples

LOOSE: *Desmond gave Molly a diamond ring.*

PERIODIC: *Shyly, anxiously, and with tears in his eyes, Desmond gave Molly a diamond ring.*

EXERCISES

1. Join these sentences, using verbal phrases, rather than subordinates.

   a. Apparently Rosa thought Gabriel's comments were insulting. She got angry at him, and she threw a pillow in his face.
   b. Bertram settled into life without a full-time job. He started spending the day in shopping malls. At last he found himself standing in soup lines and begging on street corners.
   c. The Elvis impersonators were disappointed that none of them won the talent contest. They felt let down and dejected. So the next day they decided to form a union to protect their rights.

2. Rewrite these sentences using absolutes, rather than dependent clauses.

   a. With house prices that are rising and interest rates that continue to skyrocket, prospective home buyers are looking for smaller homes, most of them needing renovation.
   b. When he spotted his missing grand-daughter, Charles sighed in relief.
   c. George fled the kitchen in a panic, leaving his dinner uneaten on the table.

3. Rewrite these simple sentences to form complex sentences.

   a. The socialites were bored. They took the stretch limousine out for a cruise. They stopped at the nearest Burger King. They watched the passersby stare at the shaded windows.
   b. Herman wanted revenge. He dragged Cleo through the city streets all day in the blazing sun.
   c. Morgan knew the painting was worth a fortune. He offered Neil $100 for it and planned to live in the Riviera on the proceeds.

4. Take the following loose sentences and make them periodic. Add complications to the subject or to the verb, or change the word order to delay the impact of the sentence.

a. The bus ground to a halt.
b. The real problem with education in this country today is that no one can afford to buy books.
c. Jumbo crossed the railroad tracks.

5. Analyze an essay that you have recently written, or are writing, to determine what sentence patterns you use most commonly. Rewrite some of the sentences, and examine the changes in emphasis that such revision creates.

6. Analyze some writing by an author you admire. Try to model some sentences on the structure of those you find.

◼ Parallelism

Parallelism is one of the basic components of good writing style. The repetitive rhythm of parallel structure allows the reader to anticipate what comes next and to keep the overall construction in mind. Consider the following sentences:

> NOT PARALLEL: *Dawn finished her essay by staying up all night, working without a break, and finally, she asked her mother to type the paper for her.*

> PARALLEL: *Dawn finished her essay by staying up all night, working without a break, and finally, asking her mother to type the paper for her.*

Making sentences that are logical, powerful and easy to understand requires a developed sense of parallel construction. To sharpen this sense, you need to become aware of certain basic requirements of balanced sentence structure.

1. Make sure grammatical elements match.

To form a parallel construction, join nouns with nouns, verbs with verbs, participles with participles, adjectives with adjectives, and so on. Connecting words like "and," "or," "but," "yet" are often signals of the need for a parallel construction.

> NOT PARALLEL: *The actor was handsome, articulate, and he loved to look at himself in a mirror.*

> PARALLEL: *The actor was handsome, articulate, and vain, loving to look at himself in a mirror.*

Since the first two items are adjectives ("handsome" and "articulate"), the last item in the series should be an adjective too.

> NOT PARALLEL: *People who are in debt should give up credit cards, borrowing money, eating out in expensive restaurants, and living above their means.*

> PARALLEL: *People who are in debt should give up using credit cards, borrowing money, eating out in expensive restaurants, and living above their means.*

The parallelism is improved when each of the nouns in question is preceded by an "ing" form.

> NOT PARALLEL: *They divorced because the husband thought that no one should read while he was talking, and the wife thought that while she was reading, no one should talk.*

PARALLEL: *They divorced because the husband thought that no one should read while he was talking, and the wife thought that no one should talk while she was reading.*

The balance is improved by maintaining the same word order in each clause.

2. Use parallel constructions after "than" or "as."

NOT PARALLEL: *It is better to light a candle than curse the darkness.*

PARALLEL: *It is better to light a candle than to curse the darkness.*

What follows "than" should be parallel with what precedes. Hence, the word "to" should be repeated.

NOT PARALLEL: *My grades are just as good as Stephanie.*

PARALLEL: *My grades are just as good as Stephanie's.*

OR: *My grades are just as good as Stephanie's grades are.*

The grades are being compared, not the grades and Stephanie.

3. Balance sentence elements connected by correlatives.

Correlatives come in pairs. They include "not only . . . but also," "both . . . and," "either . . . or," "neither . . . nor," "whether . . . or."
The grammatical constructions that follow the first co-ordinator should also follow the second.

NOT PARALLEL: *Derek didn't only apologize to her and admit that he had been wrong, he gave her a red rose and asked her forgiveness.*

PARALLEL: *Not only did Derek apologize to her and admit that he had been wrong, but he also gave her a red rose and asked her forgiveness.*

Correlative conjunctions are used here to join two clauses.

NOT PARALLEL: *Whether you take the bus or if you go by plane, two days is not long enough for a trip to Disneyland.*

PARALLEL: *Whether you take the bus or go by plane, two days is not long enough for a trip to Disneyland.*

Correlatives are used here to join two main clauses. Note the revisions in the following sentences:

NOT PARALLEL: *Arnold was sound both mentally and in body.*

PARALLEL: *Arnold was sound both in mind and in body.*

What follows "both" should be grammatically parallel to what follows "and."

NOT PARALLEL: *You either give Jason his toy back, or I'll tell your mother.*

PARALLEL: *Either you give Jason his toy back, or I'll tell your mother.*

What follows "either" must be grammatically parallel to what follows "or." In this case, a subject and verb follow both items.

4. **Parallel constructions may also be indicated by transitional signposts such as "first," "second," and "third."**

NOT PARALLEL: *The sales clerk quit his job: first, the customers were rude; second, he was tired of minimum wage; and third, disgusted at having to work on Saturday nights.*

PARALLEL: *The sales clerk quit his job: first, the customers were rude; second, he was tired of minimum wage; and third, he was disgusted at having to work on Saturday nights.*

5. **Make sure that items in a list are grammatically parallel.**

NOT PARALLEL: *This report makes four recommendations:*
1. divers should be certified by an accredited school
2. they should wear appropriate equipment at all times.
3. they should work in pairs
4. regular health checkups

PARALLEL: *This report makes four recommendations:*
1. divers should be certified by an accredited school
2. they should wear appropriate equipment at all times
3. they should work in pairs
4. they should get regular health checkups.

In this case, the items listed have been changed so that they are all main clauses; in the incorrect example, the fourth item is a phrase.

Remember that parallel construction need not be confined to words and phrases; it may extend to subordinate clauses and to sentences. Effective use of parallel structure will enhance your writing by making it clear, balanced, and carefully structured.

NOT PARALLEL: *Every one of these buildings, public and private, restored or dilapidated, will share a similar fate: bought by a developer, or if the city expands, they will be destroyed.*

PARALLEL: *Every one of these buildings, public and private, restored or dilapidated, will share a similar fate: if a developer buys them, or if the city expands, they will be destroyed.*

"Or" in the corrected sentence joins two subordinate clauses both in the active voice.

EXERCISE

Correct any faulty parallelism you find in the following sentences:

1. The lawyer listed his credentials as estate planning, pleading cases, and wheedling to get his shifty clients off the hook.
2. You either cut up your credit card, or your bank account will be a thing of the past.
3. Buy the home-entertainment centre now, and you can pay for it later.
4. Phil Donahue's advice is as relevant to the situation as Ann Landers.
5. To get a peaceful night's sleep, his mother either made him warm milk, hot chocolate, or Scotch and soda.

6. Ivana contributed to the children's fund, made a donation to Save the Rainforest in Brazil, gathered tinned goods to distribute to the poor, and a mink stole to wear to her neighbours' house party.
7. On his weekend pass, Jurgen went to the museum, to the art gallery, and visited the alligators at the zoo.
8. Marilyn not only dislikes blue cheese, but also the walnuts that were used in the tarts.
9. The business consultants spent their days stuffing envelopes, licking stamps, and they dreamed about all the money they would make.
10. Roseanne and John were burnt by the sun, overwhelmed by the great outdoors, and the blackflies bit them.

■ Active and Passive Voice

The voice of a verb tells you whether the subject acts or is acted upon. There are two voices: active and passive. In the active voice, the sentence takes this form: actor, verb, receiver. In the passive voice, the form is inverted: receiver, verb, actor, and the verb always includes some form of "to be."

In an active sentence, the subject is the actor:

The zookeeper fed the lion raw meat.

In a passive sentence, the subject is acted upon:

The raw meat was fed to the lion by the zookeeper.

Keep these points in mind when you decide which voice is more appropriate in a given context:

1. **The active voice is more forthright and usually more concise.**
2. **The active voice emphasizes the actor; the passive voice emphasizes the receiver of an action. In the example above, the zookeeper is the subject in the active sample; the raw meat is the subject in the passive sample.**
3. **The active voice emphasizes action; the passive is best used to describe stasis.**

   ACTIVE: *The pit bull terrier bit the postman.*

   PASSIVE: *The postman was bitten by the pit bull terrier.*

4. **The passive voice is awkward when it is used to avoid direct phrasing or when it results in unclear, lengthy constructions.**

   ACTIVE: *Amos, the shifty used car dealer, sold fifty lemons last month.* (direct)

   PASSIVE: *Last month, fifty lemons were sold.* (indirect: this rather dishonest use of the passive voice is typical of writers who wish to avoid responsibility for something or who wish to keep things impersonal)

   ACTIVE: *At Hallowe'en, Harry played a prank on his mother.* (clear)

   PASSIVE: *At Hallowe'en, a prank was played on his mother by Harry.* (unclear and lengthy)

5. **The passive voice is occasionally useful to avoid overuse of the pronoun "I." Be wary of overuse of the passive voice, however.**

ACTIVE: *I based this study on interviews with computer operators across the country.*

PASSIVE: *This study is based on interviews with computer operators across the country.*

6. **Remember that the passive voice is useful when you wish to emphasize the receiver of the action, rather than the performer.**

ACTIVE: *The spectators could see the fireworks for miles.*

PASSIVE: *The fireworks could be seen for miles.*

Since it is unimportant who could see the fireworks, the passive is preferable here.

7. **The passive voice is also the best choice when you wish to avoid being too personal.**

ACTIVE: *You must obey this summons immediately.*

PASSIVE: *This summons must be obeyed immediately.*

Since the summons is meant to be formal and impersonal, the passive is preferable here.

EXERCISE

Identify each of the following sentences as active or passive. Where appropriate, rewrite them by changing them from passive to active or from active to passive. Some may be fine as they are.

1. The boring class was skipped by the student who thought his time was wasted by it.
2. Hiring members of your own family is forbidden by laws against nepotism, so his old drinking buddy was hired by the head of the department instead.
3. *The Handmaid's Tale*, which was written by Margaret Atwood, was made into a feature film.
4. The scene of the crime was scrupulously examined for fingerprints.
5. The bowlegged child in the baby pictures was laughed at by her adoring relatives.
6. Many people have blamed the corruption of TV evangelism for a decline in charitable contributions.
7. The light beer was drunk from cans by the attractive people posing on the dock in the lifestyle commercial.
8. The dumping of garbage from urban areas was opposed by the irate citizens of small towns across Canada.
9. The watercolour seascape, hanging on the wall, depicts bats crossing Lake Huron and was painted by a dear friend of mine.
10. Wanda's entire paycheque every week was squandered on birdseed, herbal tea, and wildlife magazines.

Reducing Wordiness

> I have written over—often several times—
> every word I have ever published. My pencils
> outlast their erasers.
>
> *Vladimir Nabokov*

A wordy essay does not necessarily transgress the word limit of the assignment. Rather, it contains extraneous words that contribute nothing to the meaning and drain force from the essay's argument. Wordy writing is often characteristic of a first draft. It is close to idle chat: though spontaneous and sometimes even fascinating, it lacks direction. It wanders, perhaps arriving eventually at meaning; it does not set out in orderly pursuit of it. A wordy essay is often a sign of poorly revised and overdressed thought.

Make every word fit. If you can make your writing more succinct, your work will be clearer, and your reader will be more attentive. A few suggestions for improving the conciseness of your writing are listed below.

■ A Perfect Fit

Avoid visible seams

When talking, we commonly join ideas together randomly. Speed is the goal, not beautiful construction. Consider the following example:

Example

Emilio bought the book.

You decide to add a further detail.

Emilio bought the book, which was reputed to be steamy and sensational.

Your new thought shows an obvious seam. "Which" and "that" can often be removed to produce a more graceful line.

Emilio bought the book, reputed to be steamy and sensational.

Avoid frills

Often, a speaker describes something by using words accompanied by adverbs meant to accentuate their effect. Here are some examples:

X   *quite elegant*
X   *very angry*
X   *rather uneasy*

Replace these with stronger, less wordy, expressions:

- ✔ *splendid*
- ✔ *irate*
- ✔ *anxious*

In writing, the search for impact is better served by a stronger word, rather than a modified word. And, in writing, there is time to search for it. Use that time to dress your thoughts appropriately.

The same advice holds true for redundant wording. Avoid phrases like these:

- X *past history*
- X *triangular in shape*
- X *refer back*

Use these instead:

- ✔ *history*
- ✔ *triangular*
- ✔ *refer*

In each case, the omitted words added nothing to the meaning.

Avoid baggy constructions

A baggy sentence often contains vague words intended to conceal vague thoughts. Such sentences invariably include the following all-too-common words and phrases. Some of these can be excised. Most can be replaced by a single word.

X *due to the fact that*	✔ *because*
X *during the time that*	✔ *when*
X *with regard to*	✔ *about*
X *being*	(omit)

Tentative language and unnecessary compound verbs are another frequent cause of bagginess. Avoid phrases like the following:

- X *make assumptions about*
- X *come to the conclusion that*
- X *exhibit a tendency to*

Substitute:

- ✔ *assume*
- ✔ *conclude*
- ✔ *tend*

Avoid the "grand style"

Writing in the "grand style" uses pompous phrasing to clothe humble ideas. Pompous introductions are a common source of the problem:

- X *It is this theory which needs . . .*
- ✔ *This theory needs . . .*
- X *It was his view that . . .*
- ✔ *He thought that . . .*

Avoid excessive formality

Just as you wouldn't wear evening dress to compete in a bowling tournament, so you should not use static language to describe active thoughts.

Where possible, keep sentences in their typical order—use the active voice, and move from subject to verb to object. "The Prime Minister gave the order" is a much more direct statement than the passive construction, "The order was given by the Prime Minister."

X   *A decision was made by the committee to conduct further studies.*
✔   *The committee decided to conduct further studies.*

While the passive mode has its uses (as discussed earlier), it *is* wordier, less forceful, and generally harder to understand. It is all talk and no action. When revising, keep a watchful eye on the number of times you resort to the static passive voice. It can occasionally serve as a tactful way of avoiding direct confrontation.

Example

PASSIVE: *This amount is owing.* (what the bill says)

ACTIVE: *You owe us this amount.* (what the bill means)

■ Wordiness Analyzed

The preceding examples illustrate that wordiness is most often caused by speech habits not entirely abandoned in writing. To analyze the causes of your own wordiness, note especially any words you use to *warm up* as you begin to write, to *cover up* your insecurities and uncertainties as you proceed, or to *spruce up* a thought better left unadorned.

■ Preventive Measures

When editing, check to see that your sentences are designed for simplicity, concreteness, action, grace, and impact.

EXERCISE

Improve the following sentences by eliminating redundant words or phrases.
1. Kathleen teased Russell about his attitude toward storing groceries: you had to make an examination of every shelf in the refrigerator to find the milk and eggs, but the whiskey was always in plain sight.
2. In the event that Nancy's chimney was inhabited by a bat, we would have had to make a call to the wildlife foundation, but because we were in a position to say that a raccoon was living there, we made a decision not to light any fires this winter.
3. Dark blue paint exhibits a tendency to show through lighter colours, even after four coats are applied, as my past experience shows.

4. Just because Jehane and Fannie made an agreement to collaborate together on the cookbook, we should not make assumptions about our chances of being asked to dinner on a regular basis.
5. I myself feel personally that behaviour of an unfriendly nature just serves to alienate anyone in close proximity to you.
6. Ernest taught me all the basic fundamentals of the rowboat that we used throughout the summer season when we made our annual visit to the cottage, but however, our trips finally ended when the boat sprang a leak, and we got soaked to the skin.
7. The book club that they organized for the purpose of intellectual discussion possibly might have been a success after a period of time, but its general custom was to gather together to perform an analysis of the people who did not show up and to give primary consideration to what food was currently being served.
8. Albert reported to the effect that a major breakthrough had occurred: mice had, without overexaggeration, been successfully cloned despite the fact that the general public had reached the conclusion that such experiments were morally reprehensible.
9. First of all, Giovanni made a study of chandeliers in Europe, on official business: together at the same time, he took tours of historic sites and made observations of the local residents.
10. Do you want me to spell it out in detail? The sum total of everything I own (estimated roughly at $150) has been totally eradicated in order that we may have more empty space in the apartment.

Choosing Words

> Words pick up flavors and odors like butter in a
> refrigerator.
>
> *John Steinbeck*

Word choice is perhaps the most accurate index of the status of a writer. The words you choose depend in part on the role you mean to play in relation to the reader.

Example

A memo from a superior might read:

> *Vacation times will be reduced from three weeks to two weeks to accommodate increased demand.*

The effect of such impersonal language is to distance the boss from the employee; although the boss may sign the memo, there is no suggestion in the language itself that the words come from him or her.

Alternate Example

Say that you receive a letter addressed directly to you with the following message:

> *Dear Employee: I will be reducing your vacation time from three weeks to two weeks to accommodate increasing demand. Signed, The Boss.*

Although the import of the message is the same, the impact is quite different. In this case, the order does not seem to come from "on high." This time, you might be tempted to take the note personally and demand an explanation.

Because the first note is distanced, it sounds so impersonal that you might be less inclined to resent it and more easily intimidated into submission. This is not to say that the first note is better than the second, though it would be more likely to achieve the desired result: impersonal and unchallenged control over employees.

What determines the success of a style is not its beauty or power in isolation, but its impact, the response that it gets, and the relationship it forms with the reader.

Write to impress—not to intimidate

When you write an essay, the style you seek is different from that of a boss to an employee. You should address your reader as an equal; the information you impart and the viewpoint you defend are offered as reasonable choices for readers as clear-thinking as you are.

To impress a reader, you need to show what you know and to express a willingness to share it. If your words do not allow you to share your results, because they are either too technical or too vague or carelessly chosen, you will have alienated your readers. Remember that in the formal essay, the emphasis is less upon you and the reader personally than it is upon the subject at hand: your relationship is entirely professional. But in the informal essay, your personality and that of your reader play more pronounced roles: you expect that the reader will enjoy your company.

Make yourself comfortable in the language of your subject

Determining your status, and thus the proper diction for an essay, is sometimes a great challenge. After all, you may not feel much like the equal of the professor giving a course in which you feel shaky or ill prepared. Obviously, the more conversant you become with the terminology of a discipline, the easier it will be to feel like an equal and to write a stimulating learned discussion.

Just as important, however, is the confidence with which you can play the role of an equal. Think of your paper not as just another assignment, written by a student to an instructor, but as an opportunity to speak the language of the discipline to someone who understands it.

Choose your words stylishly

The "rules" that govern diction cannot be listed here, simply because word choice depends upon context. A formal essay demands formal language, just as a formal occasion demands evening dress. Likewise, informal writing allows you more freedom in self-expression and a more casual approach.

■ Diction: Fit, Form, and Function

Choose language that satisfies the criteria of fit, form, and function for the assignment in question. What follows are some pointers on how to choose (and to revise) the language of your essays.

Observing the dress code

Paying attention to the conventions of a dress code does not mean that you must wear a uniform inhibiting all expression of personality. It means, simply, that you must conform to certain standards, happily, in this case, quite flexible standards.

Keep these guidelines in mind:

1. Fit—Does your writing suit its purpose and audience?
2. Form—Does it conform to convention?
3. Function—Does your writing make your message clear?

If the idea of conforming for the sake of conforming disturbs you, remember what the consequences of not conforming may be: perhaps being misunderstood, ignored, or considered offensive. To avoid any of these perils in your use of language and in your word choice particularly, keep these hints in mind.

Avoid over-dressed language

1. Do not use too many technical or specialized terms.

Too many terms may actually prevent your reader from seeing your underlying meaning. Technical subjects clearly demand some technical terminology, but while it is partly your task to demonstrate your ability to use terms with skill and ease, you must not use them to confuse your reader or to avoid the issues.

Example

Avoid use of these words out of their normal context.

> X "feedback"   X "output"   X "interface"

Beware of words that end in "ize" and "ization." Many are acceptable, but some are questionable recent coinages, often unnecessary and vague.

> "prioritize" Replace with "establish priorities."

2. Avoid pretentious words and constructions.

Often these pretentious constructions appear as groups of nouns, attached in such a way that the reader cannot visualize the object described. The tendency to use such abstract and depersonalized language comes partly from our desire to appear sophisticated, but the effect is rather like wearing designer labels on the outside of our clothes. Such a high-sounding style may intimidate or amuse, but it does not really communicate.

Example

> Mimi found it difficult to orientate herself in the library.

Replace "orientate" with "orient." When in doubt, check usage in a dictionary or a guide to usage.

> Irregardless of her negative attitude, Gloria got the job.

Replace "irregardless" with "regardless." "Irregardless" is nonstandard usage.

3. Avoid "flashy" words.

Sometimes a student will fervently consult a thesaurus, seeking some clever ways of varying vocabulary. Although this is a commendable practice, never forget that no two words mean exactly the same thing or have precisely the same impact. When you find a synonym, check it out in the dictionary to make sure that it means what you think it does. Make sure your words know their place.

A longer word is not necessarily a stronger word. A word selected simply "for show" may be as out of place as a diamond tiara worn with a soccer uniform. Context is the first consideration in these matters. Don't use a word just because it sounds elevated.

Example

    X   *At any time of year, upon entering this voluminous structure, one cannot help but notice the low roar of conversation as the voices of the library's patrons reverberate from one concrete wall to the other.*

How can a library be "voluminous"? Replace this word with something more suitable—like "huge" or "imposing."

Avoid sloppy language
1. Avoid slang.

There are, admittedly, times when slang fits the mood. You may, for instance, wish to draw attention to the common language for a particular term, or report some dialogue. Beware of enclosing slang in quotation marks ("swell"); it may seem forced and unnatural. Unless you are sure that slang will add colour and character to your writing, avoid it. Careless slang is sloppy and perhaps more revealing than you wish.

Example

    X   *Modern socialites must wear all the latest fashions to feel that all is truly well with their world, even though this penchant for the latest threads often causes a severe drain on their bank accounts.*

Replace "latest threads" with something that matches the tone more effectively, perhaps "stylish clothes."

2. Avoid colloquial constructions.

Colloquial constructions may include slang, but they also include language that is chatty, takes too much for granted, or is not completely clear. A carefully selected colloquial word or phrase may add unexpected life to a formal paper, but the overuse of language generally confined to speech may lead the reader to dismiss the value and importance of what you are saying.

Because you have no chance to reinforce your words with body language (a raised eyebrow, a smile, a frown), your reader will need the most precise, specific language you can possibly find. You need all the power and clarity of the words at your command.

Example

X   *Nuclear disarmament seems like a pretty good idea.*

Replace "pretty good" with something stronger, perhaps the word "desirable."

3.   Avoid saying the obvious, especially in a hackneyed way.

What you have to say may not be entirely new, but your approach to the subject should be fresh, and your way of expressing yourself should give the reader a new angle of perception.

Avoid language deadened by overuse, whether it be jargon or cliché. Use language that enlightens, that sparks thought, that provokes discussion, that wakes up your reader. Saying the same old thing in the same old way may be the easy way out, but it will not have the same impact that a thoughtful or inventive use of words may have.

The cliché does, however, have its place. For instance, in the paragraph above, the phrase "the easy way out," is a cliché. In the midst of some fairly abstract prose, its presence can startle just because it is a different kind of language than what precedes it. Use clichés sparingly, and don't use them thoughtlessly. Otherwise they may have all the impact of a joke too often repeated.

Example

X   *Breed registries and associations are in the business of singing their animals'*
praises, so read their publications critically, if you are planning to buy a horse.

Replace "singing their animals' praises" with fresher, more thoughtful phrasing, perhaps "overstating the qualities of their animals."

EXERCISES

1.   Make a list of common expressions we use to describe death. (The list should include such phrases as "pushing up daisies.") Analyze these expressions to determine why they are so common. Do the same thing with words and expressions we use to describe eating.

2.   Find clichés that might be used to make the following statements.

    a. You're angry.
    b. I'm crying.
    c. He has hurt me.
    d. I've been working very hard.
    e. She drank too much.
    f. We are very tired.
    g. They are disgusted.

3. Clichés often take the form of comparisons. It was "as right as rain" or "as fresh as a daisy." Make a list of these expressions, and then vary them by drawing new comparisons.

4. Look up a common adjective in a thesaurus, and note five of the variations listed as synonyms. Check each of them in the dictionary to discover the distinctions between them, and use each of them in a sentence that makes the word's special meaning clear. Try these words:

   a. pretty
   b. ugly
   c. wicked
   d. powerful
   e. important

5. Read over essays you have written, and note any clichés or jargon you have used. Try to rephrase them in fresh language.

Documenting — MLA, APA, and University of Chicago Guidelines

Your bibliography should list all items that you quote, paraphrase, or use as source material. Three basic styles of documentation will be covered in this section: MLA style, most commonly used in the humanities; APA style, often used in the social sciences; and University of Chicago style, often used in history and other disciplines that prefer a traditional footnotes (or endnote) style.

■ Sample Bibliographical Entries in MLA Style

The examples that follow show how certain entries would appear in a bibliography, if you follow the guidelines of the Modern Language Association. These entries should serve as models when you prepare your own bibliography page. In MLA style, this page is called "Works Cited." If you need further information, consult: Joseph Gibaldi and Walter S. Achtert, *MLA Handbook for Writers of Research Papers.* 3rd ed. (New York: Modern Language Association, 1988).

Books

One author:
Frazer, James George. The Golden Bough: A Study in Magic and Religion. New York: Macmillan, 1922.

Use a shortened version of the publisher's name (in this case, Macmillan Publishing Company), making sure that your label is still recognizable. Include complete subtitles in bibliographical entries, and underline title and subtitle continuously.

Two authors and edition after the first:
Strunk, William, Jr., and E. B. White. The Elements of Style. 3rd ed. New York: Macmillan, 1979.

Three authors:
Bercuson, David, J. L. Granatstein, and W. R. Young. Sacred Trust? Brian Mulroney and the Conservative Party in Power. Toronto: Doubleday, 1986.

More than three authors:
Cornell, Paul G., et al. <u>Canada: Unity in Diversity</u>. Toronto: Holt, 1967.

Corporate author:
Imperial Oil Limited. <u>The Review</u>. Toronto: Imperial Oil, Spring 1987.

Editor:
Drabble, Margaret, ed. <u>The Oxford Companion to English Literature</u>. 5th ed. Oxford: Oxford UP, 1985.

Government publication:
Canada. Minister of Supply and Services Canada. <u>Canada Year Book 1985</u>. Ottawa: Statistics Canada, 1985.

Story or article from an anthology:
Ludwig, Jack. "The Calgary Stampede." <u>Active Voice: An Anthology of Canadian, American and Commonwealth Prose</u>. Eds. W. H. New and W. E. Messenger. Scarborough: Prentice-Hall, 1980. 111-20.

Translation:
Ringuet. <u>Thirty Acres</u>. Trans. Felix and Dorothea Walker. Toronto: McClelland and Stewart, 1960.

Reprint:
Montgomery, L. M. <u>Anne of Green Gables</u>. 1908. Toronto: McGraw-Hill, 1968.

The original hardcover edition was published in 1908. The paperback version appeared in 1968.

A work in more than one volume:
Rollins, Hyder Edward, ed. <u>The Letters of John Keats: 1814-1821</u>. 2 vols. Cambridge: Harvard UP, 1958.

A work in a series:
Woodman, Ross. <u>James Reaney</u>. Canadian Writers New Canadian Library 12. Toronto: McClelland, 1971.

The volume number is given in Arabic numerals and without the abbreviation *vol.*

Magazines, newspapers, and journals

Unsigned article:
"Students again face tight housing market." <u>The London Free Press</u> 16 Aug. 1986: C2.

The names of months other than May, June, and July are usually abbreviated. "C2" refers to the section and page number of the newspaper.

Daily newspapers:
Matyas, Joe. "Grandmother new church moderator." <u>The London Free Press</u> 16 Aug. 1986: A1.

When not part of the newspaper's name, the city's name should be given in brackets after the title.

Weekly magazine or newspaper:
Steacy, Anne, and Ben Barber. "Losing the race against drug dealers." <u>Maclean's</u> 18 Aug. 1986: 46.

Monthly or bi-monthly magazine:
Brown, Andrew. "The Freedom Portfolio." <u>Your Money</u> May-June 1986: 61-62.

Journal—continuous pagination through the year:
Campbell, Jane. " 'Competing Towers of Babel': Some Patterns of Language in <u>Hard Times</u>." <u>English Studies in Canada</u> 10.4 (1984), 416-35.

When the pages of a journal are numbered consecutively through the year, a comma precedes the page reference. Note also that an issue number ("4" in this case) follows the volume number "10." They are separated by a period.

Journal—separate pagination for each issue:
Little, Jean. "A long distance friendship." <u>Canadian Children's Literature</u> 34 (1984): 23-30.

When the pages of a journal are numbered separately for each issue, a colon precedes the page reference.

Editorial:
"Considering Refugees." Editorial. <u>The Globe and Mail</u> 7 May 1987: A6.

Book review:
Miller, J. R. Rev. of <u>The Man from Halifax: Sir John Thompson, Prime Minister</u>, by P. B. Waite. <u>Queen's Quarterly</u> 93 (1986): 646-8.

Encyclopedia
Signed with name or initials:
So[utham], B[rian] C. "Austen, Jane." <u>Encyclopaedia Britannica: Macropaedia</u>. 1974 ed.

This article appears with the initials "B.C. So." appended to it. To identify it, you need only check the index of the encyclopedia and enclose the added information in brackets.

Unsigned:
"Canadian Football League." <u>Encyclopaedia Britannica: Micropaedia</u>. 1974 ed.

Pamphlets, bulletins, and reports
Canada. Veterans Affairs Canada. <u>A Day of Remembrance</u>. Ottawa: Government of Canada, 1984.

Unpublished dissertations

DuBroy, Michael Thomas. "The Tale of the Folk: Revolution and the Late Prose Romances of William Morris." Diss. U of Western Ontario, 1982.

Micropublications

Books or periodicals in microprint form are documented as they would be in their original form.

Non-print sources

Motion picture:

My Financial Career. National Film Board. 1962.

Television or radio program:

"Family and Survival." Phil Donahue Examines The Human Animal. NBC. WICU, Erie, PA. 15 Aug. 1986.

Television interview:

Burgess, Anthony. Interview by Daniel Richler. The Journal. CBC-CFPL, London. 13 Apr. 1987.

Performance of stage play:

Pericles. By William Shakespeare. Stratford Festival Theatre. Stratford. 6 July 1986.

Recording:

Kunzel, Erich. Kunzel on Broadway: Erich Kunzel Conducting the Winnipeg Symphony Orchestra. Fanfare, DFL-9017, Toronto, 1985.

Lecture:

Gedalof, Allan. "Mystery Writing." U.W.O. Senior Alumni Series. Wesanne McKellar Room, U of Western Ontario, London, Ontario. 14 Apr. 1987.

Interview:

Wiseman, Adele. Personal Interview. 15 Apr. 1987.

For examples of citations of other non-print sources—games, globes, filmstrips, microscope slides, and transparencies—consult Eugene B. Fleischer's *A Style Manual for Citing Microform and Nonprint Media* (Chicago: American Library Association, 1978).

■ Citing Sources in MLA Style

Whenever you refer to material from another source, whether book, journal article, motion picture, or recording, you must acknowledge your source. Citing your sources no longer necessitates footnotes or endnotes. Instead, citations of sources are placed in the body of the essay in parentheses. A footnote or endnote is only necessary if you have supplementary material to add that does not properly belong in the text of the essay itself.

Simple citation

Include in parentheses after the citation only what is essential to guide the reader to the correct entry in the list of "Works Cited." Often, all that will be needed is the last name of the author followed by a page number. For example, if you were quoting from Margaret Laurence's *The Diviners*, the citation in the text would look like this:

> *Morag's collection of photographs gives the reader insight into her own hidden past. As she says, "I keep the snapshots not for what they show but for what is hidden in them" (Laurence 6).*

This citation refers the reader to the following entry on the "Works Cited" page:

> *Laurence, Margaret.* The Diviners. *Toronto: Bantam, 1974.*

If this is the only entry listed under Laurence, there is no confusion, and the reader knows that the quotation can be found on page 6 of the listed text.

Citation of more than one work by the same author

If, on the other hand, there are references to two works by the same author, a more specific notation is required. Say that you referred in the same essay to Margaret Laurence's earlier novel, *A Jest of God*. You might, perhaps, make the following reference:

> *Rachel discovers her own capacity to hide the truth from herself. As she explains, "There is room enough in anyone's bonehouse for too much duplicity" (Laurence Jest 182).*

This reference makes it clear that more than one book by Laurence is listed in "Works Cited."

Citation of a work in more than one volume

If, in an essay about Keats's poetry, you decide to quote from the two-volume collection of Keats's letters, the citation would read as follows:

> *Keats, in the composition of the odes, dedicates himself to the search for "the true voice of feeling" (Letters 2:167).*

Here the Arabic numeral 2 refers to the second volume of the letters. A colon is used to separate the volume number from the page number.

Similar adjustments must be made to clarify abbreviated citations. Always remember to ask yourself what the reader needs to know in order to find the reference easily.

Citation of poetry and of long or short quotations

Avoid redundant citations. If the body of your essay already explains the source adequately, do not restate the information in parentheses. For example, you might write the following analysis of Keats's poetry:

> *The poet speaks of the lure of death in "Ode to a Nightingale":*
>
> *Darkling I listen; and, for many a time*
> *   I have been half in love with easeful Death,*
> *Call'd him soft names in many a mused rhyme,*
> *   To take into the air my quiet breath. (51-54)*

Here only the line numbers are listed in parentheses, since the title of the poem is given in the body of the essay itself. Note, too, that a long quotation is double-spaced, indented and written without quotation marks. Because the quoted matter is poetry, the lines are given as they are in the text. If the quotation were only two lines long, it would be written in the body of the essay in the following way, using quotation marks:

> The poet speaks of the lure of death in "Ode to a Nightingale": "Darkling I listen; and, for many a time/I have been half in love with easeful Death" (51-52).

Citation of poetic drama

A reference to a play must refer to act, scene, and line numbers, as in the following case:

> In Shakespeare's A Midsummer Night's Dream, Titania, enchanted with Bottom, sees the world around with romantic eyes. As she says,
>
> > The moon methinks looks with a watery eye;
> > And when she weeps, weeps every little flower,
> > Lamenting some enforced chastity. (3.1.202-04)

Punctuation of citations

Note that for citations within the text, punctuation appears *after* the parentheses. In quotations set off from the text, citations *follow* the final punctuation. To make citations as unobtrusive as possible, try to place them at the end, rather than in the middle, of sentences.

■ Sample Bibliographic Entries in APA Style

The following entries are arranged according to the style of the *Publication Manual of the American Psychological Association*. In this case, the bibliography is given the heading References. For further details on this style of documentation, consult: American Psychological Association, *Publication Manual of the American Psychological Association*. 3rd ed. (Washington: American Psychological Assn., 1983).

Books
One Author:
Selye, H. (1956). The stress of life. New York: McGraw-Hill.

Two authors:
Gatchel, R., and Baum, A. (1983). An introduction to health psychology. Reading, MA: Addison-Wesley.

Journals
One author:
Turner, J. (1981). Social support as a contingency in psychological well-being. Journal of Health and Social Behavior, 22, 357-67.

Multiple authors:

Turner, J., Frankel, G., & Levin, D. (1983). Social support: Conceptualization, measurement, and implications for mental health. <u>Research in Community and Mental Health</u>, <u>3</u>, 67-111.

■ Citing Sources in APA Style

As with the MLA style of documentation, you may cite your sources in parentheses in APA style. In APA style, however, the year of publication is given with the author's last name; hence, the title of a work is not usually needed. Note details in the following examples:

Short Quotation:

Social support is defined as "those relationships among people that provide not only material help and emotional assurance, but also the sense that one is a continuing object of concern on the part of other people" (Pilsuk, 1982, p. 20).

Long Quotation:

Seligman (1975) argues that helplessness may lead to depression:

> *Those people who are particularly susceptible to depression may have had lives relatively devoid of mastery; their lives may have been full of situations in which they were helpless to influence the sources of suffering and relief. (p. 104)*

Note that, in this passage, the author's last name and the date of publication are not included in parentheses because they are already given in the body of the essay.

Paraphrase:

Cobb (1976) insists that stress, not social support, is the key to understanding changes in health. Social support only acts as a buffer.

Following these basic guidelines should help you assemble your notes and your bibliography with relative ease. Remember these guidelines as you prepare the documentation for your essay:

1. Be consistent.
2. Give your reader all the information needed to find a reference.
3. Check the sample research essay in this guide for a model of MLA format.
4. Check the appropriate style guide for further details.

■ Sample Bibliographic Entries in University of Chicago Style

Some disciplines, in particular history and political science, prefer a traditional footnoting style. The best source of information about this style are Kate Turabian's *A Manual for Writers* and *The Chicago Manual of Style*. The most recent editions of these works are listed in the Appendix.

If your instructor advises you to use this traditional style, rather than the parenthetical forms just outlined, refer to this section.

Since bibliographic listings can be complex, try to include as much information as possible in each entry. Remember that you are trying to help your reader locate the sources.

Books
One author:
Miller, J. S. Skyscrapers Hide the Heavens: A History of Indian-White Relations in Canada. Toronto: University of Toronto Press, 1989.

Two authors and component part in a larger work:
Rogers, E. S., and Tobobondung, Flora. "Parry Sound Farmers: A Period of Change in the Way of Life of the Algonkians of Southern Ontario." In Contributions to Canadian Ethnology, edited by David Brez Carlisle. Ottawa: National Museums of Canada, 1975.

More than three authors:
Martin, Nancy, Pat D'Arcy, Bryan Newton, and Robert Parker. Writing and Learning Across the Curriculum 11-16. Upper Montclair, N. J.: Boynton/Cook, 1976.

Note that it would be permissible to shorten the note form of this entry to read:

[1]Nancy Martin and others, Writing and Learning Across the Curriculum 11-16 (Upper Montclair, N.J.: Boynton/Cook, 1976), 50.

Edition after the first:
Barker, Larry L. Communication. 4th ed. Englewood Cliffs, N.J.: Prentice-Hall, 1987.

Association author and reprint:
Nin.Da.Waab.Jig. Minishenhying Anishnaabe-aki Walpole Island: The Soul of Indian Territory. Windsor: Commercial Associates/ Ross Roy Ltd., 1987; reprint, 1989.

This book is by a native community, and the title is in Ojibwa. The name of the community is listed first.

It is important to list information about a reprint, in case changes have been made to the pagination.

Editor:
Storr, Anthony, ed. The Essential Jung. Selected and Introduced by Anthony Storr. Princeton, N.J.: Princeton University Press, 1983.

Translation:
Pushkin, Alexander. Eugene Onegin. Trans. by Charles Johnston with an Introduction by John Bayley. Harmondsworth, Middlesex: Penguin, 1977.

A work in more than one volume:

Campbell, Joseph. <u>The Masks of God</u>. 4 vols. New York: Viking Press, 1960-68.

A work in a series:

Stanley, George F. G. <u>The War of 1812: Land Operations</u>. Canadian War Museum Historical Publication, no. 18. Toronto: Macmillan, 1983.

Component part by one author in a work by another:

Purvis, Jane. "The Experience of Schooling for Working-Class Boys and Girls in Nineteenth Century England." In <u>Defining the Curriculum: Histories and Ethnographies</u>, edited by Ivor F. Goodson and Stephen J. Ball, 89-115. London: Falmer Press, 1984.

Magazines, newspapers, and journals

Article in a popular magazine:

Mohr, Merilyn. "The Evolutionary Image." <u>Equinox</u>, March/April 1989, 80-93.

Article in a scholarly journal:

Creighton, D. G. "The Economic Background of the Rebellions of 1867." <u>The Canadian Journal of Economics and Political Science</u> 4 (1937): 322-34.

Articles in encyclopedias:

<u>Encyclopedia Britannica</u>, 1974 ed. S.V. "Friedrich Nietzsche." By Walter Kaufmann.

Newspaper:

"Feminists Demand Legal System Review." <u>London Free Press</u>, 10 February 1990, D1.

Book review:

Rugoff, Milton. "The Feminine Mystic." Review of <u>Spiritualism and Women's Rights in Nineteenth Century America</u> by Ann Braude. <u>The New York Times Book Review</u>, 14 Jan. 1990, 19.

Non-print sources

Motion picture:

Phillips, Robin. Dir. <u>The Wars</u>. Toronto: Spectra Films, 1983.

Television or radio program:

CBC. "The Nature of Things." 7 February 1990. "Thirty Years of Discovery." David Suzuki, narrator.

Published interview:

Davies, Robertson. "Interview with Robertson Davies: The Bizarre and Passionate Life of the Canadian People." Interview by Silver Donald Cameron (9 November 1971). <u>Conversations with Canadian Novelists</u>. Toronto: Colbert Agency, Inc., 1973.

Unpublished interview:
Beedle, Merle Assance. Interview by author, March 1989.

Special forms
Unpublished materials:
Crown Attorney's Case Book for Cases Prosecuted Under the Liquor Control Act (1927) in Middlesex County. Regional Room, D. B. Weldon Library, University of Western Ontario, London.

Dissertations:
Gates, David. "The Image of the Labyrinth in Some Victorian Novels." Ph.D. diss., The University of Western Ontario, 1982.

Government Publications
Here are some basic rules to follow when citing government documents.

1. List name of country, state, city, or district first in bibliographies. In notes, however, this information may be left out because it will be obvious from the text.
2. Next, list the name of the legislative body, department, or board. Use the name of the office rather than the name of the officer.
3. Follow with the name of the division or commission, if any.
4. Give the title of the document, underlined.
5. Include any additional information needed to find the document.

Canadian documents:
List Canadian documents according to the executive department that issued them (either Senate or House of Commons). Identify them by calendar year. The note would also include chapter number.

Canada. House of Commons. Order Paper and Notices. 16 February 1972.
Note Form:
[1] House of Commons, Order Paper and Notices, 16 February 1972, 6.

American documents:
U. S. Congress. Senate. Committee on Foreign Relations. Aid Programs to Developing Countries. Washington, D.C.: GPO, 1989.

Here "GPO" stands for Government Printing Office.

Note Form:
[1] U. S. Congress, Senate, Committee on Foreign Relations, Aid Programs to Developing Countries (Washington, D.C.: GPO, 1989), 7.

British documents:
U. K. Board of Education. Report of the Committee on the Position of Natural Science in the Educational System of Great Britain. London: HMSO, 1918.

Here "HMSO" stands for Her (His) Majesty's Stationery Office.

Note Form:

[1] Board of Education, <u>Report of the Committee on the Position of Natural Science in the Educational System of Great Britain</u> (London: HMSO, 1918), 6.

For more help in citing government documents, refer to

Turabian, Kate L. <u>A Manual for Writers of Term Papers</u>. 5th ed. Chicago: University of Chicago Press, 1987.

■ Citing Sources in University of Chicago Style

Although notes can be used both for commentary and for reference, this section will concentrate on their use in making reference to particular works. Remember, though, that a note is often a good place to include supplementary commentary that does not belong in your paper proper, but that needs to be included.

In the University of Chicago style of documentation, you include notes compiled at the bottom of pages (footnotes) or in a list compiled at the end of the paper (endnotes). Each entry in your notes should correspond to a number in the text of your paper. The note numbers should appear a half line above your text at the end of the passage you are quoting or paraphrasing. The first line of each note is indented eight spaces from the left margin.

When you use this traditional style of documentation, always single space your notes, and leave a space between each one.

The first note should contain complete information about the location of the source. Be sure to include everything that your reader will need to find it. Take your information from the title page of the work in question. The order of information for the first note follows this format:

For a first complete note, in this case a book
Note number above the line
Name of author(s) in formal order
Title and subtitle, if any, underlined
Name of editor or translator
Name of author of introduction, if different from author
Name or number of edition, if other than the first
Name of series in which book appears, with volume or number
Facts of publication, enclosed in parentheses:

(Place of publication: Name of publisher, Date of publication),
Page number of citation

Sometimes some of these things will not apply to the text you are citing. Occasionally, too, some of the facts of publication may be missing. These may be supplied in square brackets, if you know them, or they may be indicated by these abbreviations:

n.p. meaning "no place" or "no publisher" or both
n.d. meaning "no date"

A first full reference to a book would look like this:
[6] Northrop Frye, The Great Code: The Bible and Literature (New York: Harcourt Brace Jovanovich, 1982), p. 117.

For a first complete note, in this case an article

Follow this order for an article in a magazine or periodical:

Name of author(s)
Title of article in quotation marks
Name of periodical underlined
Volume number or issue
Publication date in parentheses
Page numbers, inclusive (These normally are not preceded by "p." for page or "pp." for pages, unless confusion is possible.)

A first full reference to an article would look like this:

[3] Peter Elbow, "Embracing Contraries in the Writing Process," College Composition and Communication, 35, 155-171.

Note that long quoted passages in University of Chicago style are single spaced and indented five spaces.

Note that there are some significant differences between the format of notes and of bibliographic entries.

1. Notes are listed consecutively by number; bibliographic entries are listed alphabetically by last name of author. Hence, authors' names are not inverted in notes, though they are in bibliographies.
2. In notes, items are usually separated with commas; in bibliographic entries, items are separated with periods.
3. Notes include facts of publication in parentheses; bibliographic entries do not.
4. Notes include the specific page references of the citation; bibliographic entries do not, though they do include the page number of journal articles, inclusive.

Notes after the first full reference to a work

The best way to cite something after the first full reference is to include the following:

Author's last name
Shortened title of the work, maintaining key words without changing word order
Page number

Note: The use of Latin abbreviations such as Ibid. is now discouraged. The second references to the book and article listed above would look like these:

[7] Frye, *Code*, 133.
[8] Elbow, "Embracing Contraries," 333.

Some instructors may allow you to dispense with a shortened version of the title and use just the author's last name and the page number. This method is used only if you are citing no more than one work by an author. In any case, check with your instructor first.

PART SIX

Reviewing
the Results

Perfecting the Essay

A poet can survive everything but a misprint.
Oscar Wilde

Even after all your hard work, some minor but significant detail may affect the reader's perception of your paper. Often these errors are the most embarrassing ones, errors that undercut your effort and distract the reader's attention from the elegance of your essay's form and the substance of its content. Like the emperor with no clothes, you and your work may be easily subjected to ridicule or to charges of arrogance if you neglect responsible proofreading and stringent self-criticism. To ensure the quality of your work, follow these steps:

1. Move from the whole to the parts.

Revising is complicated. The process involves more than superficial corrections of mechanical errors. It involves a careful reconsideration of every part of your draft. Try to follow this sequence, or one adapted to suit you, when you revise your papers.

  a. Check your facts. Does anything need to be added or changed?
  b. Rethink your scheme of organization. Does the order make sense?
  c. Test paragraph structure. Are your ideas developed and linked properly?
  d. Read over your sentences. Are they clear, smooth, varied?
  e. Examine your word choice. Is it accurate, suitable, effective?
  f. Check your grammar and spelling. Is the paper free of errors?

2. Reflect on your image.

Just as you wouldn't buy an item of clothing without first looking to see if it suited you and fit properly, don't write a paper and then submit it without first assessing its immediate impact on its readers. Reread the paper, scrutinizing its details very carefully—preferably a few days after you have written it. Reading aloud will help you find any awkward instances of grammatical construction and style. If you *still* feel insecure, ask a friend to read it too.

3. If you can't be perfect, be careful.

Some errors, in this imperfect world, may still creep in. Make necessary corrections as unobtrusively as possible. Resist the impulse to retype the whole paper (possibly introducing new errors) and instead make the corrections neatly in black ink—above the line. Stroke out unwanted letters with a small vertical line, and remove repeated words by the judicious use of "white-out" (liquid paper) or the simple horizontal stroke of a pen.

4. Make your paper "easy on the eyes."

Don't allow your essay to offend the eye. Specifically, avoid erasable bond paper (which baffles the instructor who tries to write on it). Avoid typewriter ribbon so faded that you develop eyestrain trying to read a paper typed with it. Make your handwriting bold, large, and neat. If you submit a computer printout, take special care in proofreading to avoid errors that may have been introduced in production. Submit the paper in a tidy folder, neatly stapled or paper-clipped (as your instructor may prefer). Even if neatness is not an acknowledged criterion of excellence, there is no question that first impressions have a lasting effect.

5. Tie up any loose threads.

Don't submit your paper without checking such details as page numbers, exact quotations, bibliographical information, doubtful spellings, word divisions, and grammatical constructions.

6. Follow the "dress code."

Make sure that your assignment adheres to any conditions explicitly stated by the instructor, however arbitrary or trivial such matters may seem to you. Check to see that the mechanical format of your paper conforms to the expected standards of the instructor. Such items as the treatment of abbreviations, bibliographical arrangement, even the format of the title page and the position and form of page numbers need careful attention. Although you may have already invested considerable time in these matters, a last-minute check is a good idea.

Mending the Essay

> I believe in miracles in every area of life except writing. Experience has taught me that there are no miracles in writing. The only thing that produces good writing is hard work.
>
> *Isaac Bashevis Singer*

If, when you get an essay back, you find that your work has been disappointing, there are still some things you can do to redeem yourself. It may be too late to get the kind of grade that you had in mind on this particular paper, but some of the tactics proposed below ought to make the next essay better.

First, don't throw the paper away in a fit of glee or gloom. You write essays not only to get grades but also to learn how to write. Long after you have forgotten the facts and figures involved in writing your paper, you will still have the writing skills that were developed in its preparation. Your reading, writing, and research skills are the most visible parts of your education long after you graduate.

■ Deciphering Comments

1. **Read the grader's comments when your essays are returned to you—regardless of the grade you receive.**

   Don't read only the comments accompanying the grade at the end of the paper, but also any questions or hints dropped in the margins or within the text of the paper.

2. **Next, see that you understand what the comments and questions mean.**

   The list below should help:

agr	– error in agreement (subject/verb or antecedent/pronoun)
awk	– awkward wording
case	– error in pronoun case
cs	– comma splice
D	– problem with diction
dm	– dangling modifier
doc	– error in documentation
frag	– sentence fragment
gr	– error in grammar or usage

mm	– misplaced modifier
p	– error in punctuation
par	– problem with paragraphing
pass	– overuse of the passive voice
ref	– problem with pronoun reference
rep	– repetition
run-on	– run-on sentence
shift	– shift in verb tense or logic
sp	– error in spelling
T	– error in verb tense
TS	– problem with thesis statement
trans	– transition
‖	– faulty parallelism
∧	– something missing
wdy	– problem with wordiness

3. Ask your instructor to explain a particular comment, if you do not understand it.

4. When you have read through the comments, try to analyze the kind of mistakes that you make most frequently and determine that you will take steps to eliminate them.

5. Next, consult a reliable guide in order to correct your mistakes.

Such guides include a dictionary (for spelling errors and errors of usage), a writing/grammar handbook (such as this one), or a guide to proper format of notes and bibliography (such as the *MLA Handbook*).

▪ Learning from Experience

1. Analyze the strengths and weaknesses of your style.

At first, this may seem a puzzling endeavour, but after a time you should be able to discern changes in your writing—not only in its mechanics, but in the development of its thought as well.

2. Analyze your writing habits.

Do you find that you have certain favourite expressions that crop up too often? Do your readers frequently comment that your sentences are too complex or too simple? Do certain tactics in your argument often meet with an unfavourable response? Paying attention to these trends in your collected essays will enable you to become more sensitive to your patterns of self-expression and more able to prevent problems in the future.

3. Keep a list of your most common spelling and grammar errors from past work.

Refer to this list when you are about to write the final draft of your next paper. It may help eliminate some pitfalls.

4. Exercise your writing skills.

Reading is probably not a strong enough remedy to cure you of some errors; writing is the recommended therapy. If possible, set yourself the task of completing some exercises aimed at a specific problem diagnosed by your instructor. If, for example, dangling modifiers are a persistent problem, consult the section in this book on their diagnosis and treatment. Your instructor may agree to check your answers afterwards.

5. Rewrite.

Rewriting is also a good way of curing some of the ills of essay writing. Try, for example, to recast a troublesome paragraph in clearer, smoother prose, incorporating your instructor's suggestions. Remember, though, that no writer ever developed a style mechanically; it is intimately related to thought. Rethink your thoughts as you rewrite. You will learn a great deal about the impact your writing has on its readers if you remember the grader's comments.

6. Work though appropriate sections of this book with an essay that has just been returned.

This exercise will help you in your next essay assignment.

7. Experiment.

Writing should not always be a chore. Sometimes, when you find yourself able to express something exactly the way you want to, writing becomes play. Allow yourself to become comfortable as you write. Remember that your real writing purpose, grades and completed assignments aside, is to say what you want to say. Practice will make writing a satisfying form of self-expression.

Glossary of Usage

> English usage is sometimes more than mere taste, judgment and education—sometimes it's sheer luck, like getting across a street.
>
> *E. B. White*

This glossary lists some words that are a common source of errors, either because they are confused with other words, or because they are not acceptable in standard usage. Check through this list if you are in doubt about a particular usage.

accept/except
"Accept" is a verb that means to "consent to"; "except" is a verb or a preposition that means "to exclude."

> *I would **accept** your proposition **except** for my husband and six children.*

advice/advise
"Advice" is a noun; "advise" is a verb.

> *I **advise** you to follow your mother's **advice**.*

affect/effect
"Affect" is usually a verb; "effect" is usually a noun. Note, however, that "effect" may occasionally be a verb, meaning "to bring about."

> *His break-up with his girlfriend **affected** his grade point average.*
> *A broken heart may have a bad **effect** on scholastic achievement.*
> *He thought that by writing a tear-stained letter he could perhaps **effect** a reconciliation.*

allude/elude
"To allude" means "to make indirect reference to"; "to elude" means "to escape."

> *A lewd reference may **elude** you, but it may perhaps **allude** to another literary source.*

allusion/illusion
The first is a veiled or indirect reference; the second is a deception.

> *She found the poet's **allusion** to Shakespeare; her belief that the words came from Milton was an **illusion**.*

a lot/allot
"A lot" is a colloquialism for "many" or "a great deal"; "to allot" is a verb, meaning "to divide" or "to parcel out." There is no form "alot."

> *Each of the heiresses had been **allotted a lot** of their grandfather's fortune.*

all together/altogether
The first means "in a group"; the second means "completely" or "entirely."

> **All together**, *the students in the class decided that the teacher was* **altogether** *incompetent.*

all right/alright
The *first* is the correct spelling.

among/between
"Among" involves more than two; "between" involves just two.

> **Among** *his peers he is considered a genius;* **between** *you and me, I think he is overrated.*

amount of/number of
"Amount of" is for quantities that cannot be counted and hence is followed by a singular noun; "a number of" is for quantities that may be counted and takes a plural noun.

> *A* **number** *of students drink a large* **amount** *of alcohol.*

as/because
"Because" should be used instead of "as" in a sentence meant to show cause and effect, since "as" or "while" may also refer to the passage of time.

> *X* **As** *he was awaiting trial, he refused to speak to the press.* (ambiguous)

> ✔ **Because** *he was awaiting trial, he refused to speak to the press.*

aspect
Avoid this vague word. While not always incorrect, it often contributes to vagueness.

being/being as/being that
"Being" can almost always be eliminated. "Being as" or "being that" should be replaced by "because" or "since."

bottom line
This popular bit of financial jargon has no place in formal writing.

can/may
"Can" implies ability; "may" implies permission or possibility.

> *I* **may** *go shopping today since I* **can** *buy anything I want.*

in the case of
A wordy construction, best avoided.

> *X In the* **case** *of your mother-in-law, she means well.*
> ✔ *Your mother-in-law means well.*

centre on/revolve around
Avoid "centre around," an illogical phrase.

comprises/comprised of
"Comprises" means "consists of." Do *not* use "is comprised of."

> *X Canada is comprised of ten provinces and two territories.*
> ✔ *Canada comprises ten provinces and two territories.*

conscious/conscience

"Conscious" is an adjective meaning "aware"; "conscience" is one's inner sense of morality.

*The jury became increasingly **conscious** of the criminal's lack of **conscience**.*

continual/continuous

"continual" means "repeated"; "continuous" means "without ceasing."

*Her homework was **continually** interrupted by telephone calls from vacuum cleaner salesmen.*
*The air conditioner was used **continuously** throughout the long, hot day.*

could of/should of/would of

You mean "could have," "would have."

data/criteria/phenomena/media

All of these words are plural. Their singular forms are "datum," "criterion," "phenomenon," and "medium." Check the subject and verb agreement carefully with each.

*Some people think the media **are** responsible for all modern ills.*

disinterested/uninterested

"Disinterested" means "impartial"; "uninterested" means "bored" or "unconcerned."

*The ideal referee is **disinterested** in the outcome of the game, but shouldn't be **uninterested** in the actions of the players.*

due to

"Due to" is acceptable only after some form of the verb "to be." Use "because of" to imply a causal relationship.

*The bus is **due to** arrive in fifteen minutes.*
Because of his allergies, he had to give up Muffy, his Persian cat.

elicit/illicit

"To elicit" is a verb meaning to "evoke"; "illicit" is an adjective meaning "illegal."

*The questions at the press conference should **elicit** some response to the president's **illicit** behaviour.*

enthuse/enthused

Avoid these words. Use "enthusiastic" instead.

*Bruce Springsteen's fans were **enthusiastic** about his concert tour.*

equally as

Do not use "equally" and "as" together. Instead, use one or the other

She and her brother are equally good at contact sports.
She is as good as her brother at contact sports.

etc.

Avoid this abbreviation, which usually means that the author does not know what else to say.

the fact that
Avoid this wordy expression.

factor
This word generally adds nothing; leave it out.

farther/further
"Farther" refers to actual distance; "further" is abstract.

> The **farther** he walked, the more his feet hurt.
> She would not stand for any **further** shenanigans.

fewer/less
"Fewer" is used with plural nouns; "less" is used with singular nouns.

> The **fewer** the guests, the **less** liquor we will need.

firstly, secondly,
"First" and "second" are all you really need.

hopefully
Replace this word with "It is hoped that," or more simply, I (we) hope that.

> X **Hopefully,** the paper will be finished tomorrow.

This sentence implies that the paper itself is hopeful.

> ✔ **It is hoped that** the paper will be finished tomorrow.
> ✔ **I hope** that the paper will be finished tomorrow.

impact on
"Impact" is a noun, not a verb. Replace it with "have an impact on."

> The economy will **have an impact on** workers' salaries.

imply/infer
"To imply" means "to suggest"; "to infer" means "to conclude."

> She **implied** that he was cheap; he **inferred** that he should have offered to pay her bus fare.

input
Avoid this word and other computer jargon, except when you are discussing computers.

into
Avoid using this preposition to mean "interested in."

> X He was **into** macramé.
> ✔ He was **interested in** macramé.

irregardless
The correct word is "regardless."

its/it's
"Its" is the possessive form, like "his" or "her."
"It's" is a contraction for "it is" or "it has."

> That dog's bark is worse than **its** bite.
> **It's** certainly got big teeth, though.

-ize

Avoid some of the newly created verbs with this ending. They are part of the growing and deplorable tendency to turn nouns into verbs, as in "prioritize." There is usually a simpler form.

> X He **utilized** the facilities.
> ✔ He **used** the facilities.

lay/lie

"Lay" takes an object; "lie" does not.

> The farmer made the hen **lie** on the nest to **lay** an egg.

like/as/as if

"Like" is a preposition and should not be used as a conjunction. Substitute "as" or "as if" if a clause follows.

> X He looks **like** he's going to die.
> ✔ He looks **as if** he's going to die.
> ✔ He looks **like** death warmed over.

myself

"Myself" is not a more polite form of "I" or "me." It should be reserved for use as an intensifier or reflexive.

> X The hostess introduced my wife and myself to the guests.
> ✔ The hostess introduced my wife and me to the guests.
> ✔ I, myself, solved the problem.
> ✔ I drove myself to the airport.

parameters/perimeters

Use "perimeters" to mean "boundaries," or to refer to a length or distance. Avoid the use of "parameters" except in its specific application to geometry.

parent

Do not use this word as a verb; "parenting" is also suspect. "Parenthood" is a perfectly acceptable substitute.

practice/practise

"Practice" is the noun; "practise" is the verb.

> I know **practice** makes perfect, but I hate to **practise**.

presently

Substitute "currently" or "now." "Presently" actually means "soon."

principal/principle

The first means "chief" or "main" as an adjective, the head of a school as a noun; the second means "a basic truth."

> His **principal** objection to her comments was that they were based on questionable **principles**.

quote/quotation

"Quote" is a verb, *not* a noun — "quotation" is the noun.

> X This **quote** from Richard Nixon makes the point clear.
> ✔ This **quotation** from Richard Nixon makes the point clear.

relate to

Use this verb to indicate how one idea is related to another. Do not use it to mean "get along with."

> X *How do you relate to your new psychiatrist?*
> ✔ *This point relates directly to my argument.*

suppose to

Use "supposed to," or better, use "should" or "ought to."

that/which

Use "that" when what follows restricts the meaning. Use "which" in a non-restrictive case.

> *Here is the book* **that** *I told you about.* (not just any book, but a specific one)

> *His fortune,* **which** *included stock certificates, bonds, and the first penny he had ever earned, was kept in an old shoebox under his bed.* (the words surrounded by commas supply incidental, non-restrictive information)

their/there/they're

"Their" is possessive; "there" is an adverb or an expletive; "they're" is a contraction of "they are."

> **There** *ought to be a law against* **their** *foolishness.* **They're** *asking for trouble.*

try and

Replace this phrase with "try to."

> *We must* **try to** *stop meeting like this.*

unique

"Unique" means "one of a kind." It cannot be modified.

> X *Her sequined dress was* **very unique.**
> ✔ *Her sequined dress was* **unique.**

who's/whose

"Who's" is a contraction of "who is" or "who has"; "whose" is the possessive form.

> **Who's** *been sleeping in my bed?*

> **Whose** *bed is this, anyway?*

-wise

Avoid this suffix.

> X *Timewise, the project is on schedule.*
> ✔ *The project is on schedule.*

Appendix

The following is a list of sources of general information as well as sources pertaining to specific disciplines.

■ General Dictionaries

Gage Canadian Dictionary (1983)
The Oxford English Dictionary (1888–1928, Supplements)
Webster's Third New International Dictionary (1961)

■ Special Dictionaries

Dictionary of Modern English Usage (1965)
Roget's International Thesaurus (1977)

■ General Encyclopedias

The Canadian Encyclopedia (1988)
New Encyclopaedia Britannica (1985)

■ Special Encyclopedias and Reference Works

Biography

Canadian Who's Who (1910–)
Dictionary of American Biography (1927–80, Supplements)
Dictionary of Canadian Biography (1966–)
Dictionary of National Biography (1862–1958, Supplements)
International Who's Who (1935–)
Who's Who in America (1899–)

Fine Arts

Encyclopedia of World Art (1959–83)
Encyclopedia of World Architecture (1979)

History

Canadian Historical Review
An Encyclopedia of World History (1972)
Story, N. *The Oxford Companion to Canadian History and Literature* (1967, Supplement 1973)

Literature

Bartlett, John. *Familiar Quotations* (1980)
Cambridge History of American Literature (1960)

Cambridge History of English Literature (1907–33)
Contemporary Authors (1962–)
Drabble, Margaret, ed. *The Oxford Companion to English Literature* (1985)
Essay and General Literature Index (1900–)
Granger's Index to Poetry (1982)
Hart, James D., ed. *Oxford Companion to American Literature* (1983)
Harvey, Sir Paul, ed. *Oxford Companion to Classical Literature* (1989)
New Cambridge Bibliography of English Literature (1985)
Short Story Index (1974–)
Toye, William, ed. *Oxford Companion to Canadian Literature* (1983)

Music
Encyclopedia of Music in Canada (1981)
The New Grove Dictionary of Music and Musicians (1980)
Thompson, Oscar. *International Cyclopedia of Music and Musicians* (1985)

Philosophy
Dictionary of the History of Ideas (1973–74)
Encyclopedia of Philosophy (1967)

Social science
International Encyclopedia of the Social Sciences (1968–79)
Handbook of Social Science Research (1979)
The Literature of Political Science (1969)
Sources of Information in the Social Sciences (1986)

Yearbooks (current information)
Britannica Book of the Year (1938–)
Canadian Almanac and Directory (1847–)
Canadian Annual Review (1960–)
Canadian News Facts (1967–)
Facts on File (1940–)
World Almanac and Book of Facts (1868–)

■ Periodical Indexes

Another excellent source of information is the periodical index. Often the periodical will give you more current material than is available in books. There are many indexes to supply you with the names of publications. The following list will help get you started. General indexes are indicated by a single asterisk (*). Indexes and abstracts available "on line" are indicated by double asterisks (**).

Abstracts of Popular Culture (1976–82)
**Art Index* (1929–)
American Humanities Index (1975–)
**Biography Index* (1949–)

***Book Review Digest* (1905–)
***Business Periodicals Index* (1958–)
***Canadian Business Index* (1975–)
***Canadian Magazine Index* (1985–)
* ***Canadian Periodical Index* (1928–)
**Humanities Index (1974)
　International Political Science Abstracts (1951–)
***MLA International Bibliography of Books and Articles on the Modern Languages and Literatures* (1921–)
　Music Index (1949–)
* ***New York Times Index* (1851–)
　**Poole's Index to Periodical Literature* (1802–1906) (subject guide only, but some libraries may have a separate author index)
　Popular Periodical Index (1973–)
***Psychological Abstracts* (1927–)
* ***Readers' Guide to Periodical Literature* (1900–)
* ***Social Sciences Index* (1974)
***Sociological Abstracts* (1953–)

■ Guides to Documentation

American Psychological Association. *Publication Manual of the American Psychological Association.* 3rd ed. Washington: American Psychological Assn., 1983.

The Chicago Manual of Style. 13th ed. Chicago: U of Chicago P, 1982.

Gibaldi, Joseph, and Walter S. Achtert. *MLA Handbook for Writers of Research Papers.* 3rd ed. New York: Modern Language Association, 1988.

Hodges, John C., Mary E. Whitten, Judy Brown, and Jane Flick. *Harbrace College Handbook for Canadian Writers.* 3rd ed. Toronto: Harcourt Brace Jovanovich, Canada, 1990.

Turabian, Kate L. *A Manual for Writers of Term Papers, Theses, and Dissertations.* 5th ed. Chicago: U of Chicago P, 1987.

Wiles, Roy M. *Scholarly Reporting in the Humanities.* 4th ed. Toronto: U of Toronto P, 1979.

Index

To the owner of this book:

We are interested in your reaction to *Fit to Print: The Canadian Student's Guide to Essay Writing*, Second Edition, by Joanne Buckley.

1. What was your reason for using this book?

    ____ university course   ____ continuing education course

    ____ college course   ____ personal interest

                                                         ____ other (specify)

2. In which school are you enrolled? _____

3. Approximately how much of the book did you use?

    ____ ¼   ____ ½   ____ ¾   ____ all

4. What is the best aspect of the book?

5. Have you any suggestions for improvement?

6. Is there anything that should be added?

Fold here